Boost.Asio C++ Network Programming

Second Edition

Learn effective C++ network programming
with Boost.Asio and become a proficient
C++ network programmer

Wisnu Anggoro

John Torjo

BIRMINGHAM - MUMBAI

Boost.Asio C++ Network Programming
Second Edition

First published: February 2013

Second published: September 2015

Production reference: 1100915

Published by Packt Publishing Ltd.
Livery Place
35 Livery Street
Birmingham B3 2PB, UK.

ISBN 978-1-78528-307-9

www.packtpub.com

Credits

Authors
Wisnu Anggoro
John Torjo

Reviewers
Toma Becea
Iyed Bennour
Vic Taylor

Commissioning Editor
Veena Pagare

Acquisition Editor
Tushar Gupta

Content Development Editor
Rashmi Suvarna

Technical Editor
Abhishek R. Kotian

Copy Editor
Neha Vyas

Project Coordinator
Judie Jose

Proofreader
Safis Editing

Indexer
Mariammal Chettiyar

Production Coordinator
Conidon Miranda

Cover Work
Conidon Miranda

About the Authors

Wisnu Anggoro is a Microsoft Certified Professional in C# programming and an experienced C/C++ developer. He has been programming since he was in junior high school, and he started developing computer applications using basic programming in the MS-DOS environment. He has good experience in smart card programming as well as desktop and web application programming, such as designing, developing, and supporting live use applications for SIM Card Operating System Porting, personalization, PC/SC communication, and other smart card applications that require the use of C# and C/C++.

He is currently a senior smart card software engineer at Cipta Srigati Lestari (www.cslgroup.co.id), an Indonesian company that specializes in the innovation and technology of smart cards. There, he holds the position of the smart card tools team leader. He has the responsibility of managing the smart card tools team and developing various applications and tools in order to create smart cards that can connect to any computer application.

Before this, he worked as a platform engineer at the same company. In this position, he successfully ported the GSM operating system from Tongfang THC20F17BD Chip (MCS51) to Xirka XSTSCSIM864 Chip (MCS51) and the RUIM operating system from Samsung S3FC9xx Chip (ARM) to EMTG97 Chip (MCS51). He also successfully developed a personalization tool for the MIFARE Classic card, a smart card key generator dongle used to activate the operating system based on the ICCID number using its own cryptography algorithm, and various smart card applications. He did this by accessing smart card readers using P/Invoke C#, RESTful applications that use HttpNet and JSON XML serialization in C#, and responsive applications that use multithreading and asynchronous processing in C#.

This is his first, and he plans to write as many books about C/C++ and C# programming in the future as possible. You can reach him through his e-mail at wisnu@anggoro.net.

Acknowledgements

First and foremost, I would like to thank God, whose many blessings have made me who I am today. To my wife, Vivin, for her constant love and support and for not letting me give up on writing this book. To my beloved son, Olav, who has given me so much happiness and has kept me hopping. To my parents and family for their inspiration.

Also, thank you to the following individuals; without their contributions and support, this book would not have been written.

The great team at Packt Publishing, especially Tushar Gupta, my acquisition editor, who invited me to author this book and guided me to start writing it. Rashmi Suvarna, my content development editor, for her efforts in making my book's content awesome. Abhishek Kotian, my technical editor, who ensured that all the source code is valid; thanks for correcting my confusing phrases.

My superiors at Cipta Srigati Lestari, Abdul Hakim and Benediktus Dwi Desiyanto, for all the knowledge you have shared—not only about technical stuff, but also about soft skills. It proved to be really helpful while I was writing this book.

Christopher Kohlhoff, the founder of Boost Asio; thanks for your video presentation on YouTube titled *Thinking Asynchronously: Designing Applications with Boost.Asio*, which can be found at `https://www.youtube.com/watch?v=D-lTwGJRx0o`.

Boris Schäling, the author of *The Boost C++ Libraries* and the owner of `http://www.theboostcpplibraries.com`; thanks for your site. It has inspired me a lot.

Drew Benton, thanks for sharing your knowledge of Boost.Asio on the `gamedev.net` forum at `http://www.gamedev.net/blog/950/entry-2249317-a-guide-to-getting-started-with-boostasio/?pg=1`.

Thanks to Harvard University for providing free lectures on GDB at `http://www.sourceware.org/gdb/current/onlinedocs/gdb.html` and also for providing quick and easy-to-understand videos about GDB on YouTube at `https://www.youtube.com/watch?v=sCtY--xRUyI`.

John Torjo is a renown C++ expert. He has been programming for over 15 years, most of which were spent doing C++. Sometimes, he also codes C# or Java. He's also enjoyed writing articles about programming in C++ Users Journal (currently, Dr. Dobbs) and other magazines. In his spare time, he likes playing poker and driving fast cars. One of his freelance projects lets him combine two of his passions, programming and poker. You can reach him at `john.code@torjo.com`.

About the Reviewers

Toma Becea is a passionate programmer and an employee at Macadamian Inc. He loves to delve into technologies such as WPF, WebRTC, and iOS. He also likes cycling, playing football, and hang gliding.

Iyed Bennour is a senior software engineer. He spent the last 10 years developing large-scale multithreading and networking C++ software in the telecommunication industry. He sees software development as a craft that needs to be mastered and likes to think of himself as a software craftsman.

Vic Taylor is a formally trained educator who received his PhD in urban education from the University of Wisconsin—Milwaukee in 1999. He has been programming since he fell in love with it in 1979, when he was still in graduate school (University of Wisconsin—Madison) and completing a data analysis that required him to learn enough of Fortran to use IMSL.

Vic has been a professional programmer/consultant for about 35 years now, and he has been contracted by Nevelex Corporation to write C++11 code for several DirecTV projects. Some of his previous accomplishments include single-handedly analyzing, designing, and implementing four major industrial control applications for Badger Meter Incorporated (Milwaukee, WI) on a contractual basis between 1994 and 2005.

www.PacktPub.com

Support files, eBooks, discount offers, and more

For support files and downloads related to your book, please visit www.PacktPub.com.

Did you know that Packt offers eBook versions of every book published, with PDF and ePub files available? You can upgrade to the eBook version at www.PacktPub.com and as a print book customer, you are entitled to a discount on the eBook copy. Get in touch with us at service@packtpub.com for more details.

At www.PacktPub.com, you can also read a collection of free technical articles, sign up for a range of free newsletters and receive exclusive discounts and offers on Packt books and eBooks.

https://www2.packtpub.com/books/subscription/packtlib

Do you need instant solutions to your IT questions? PacktLib is Packt's online digital book library. Here, you can search, access, and read Packt's entire library of books.

Why subscribe?

- Fully searchable across every book published by Packt
- Copy and paste, print, and bookmark content
- On demand and accessible via a web browser

Free access for Packt account holders

If you have an account with Packt at www.PacktPub.com, you can use this to access PacktLib today and view 9 entirely free books. Simply use your login credentials for immediate access.

Table of Contents

Preface

Network applications were not very easy to develop about two decades ago. But thanks to Boost.Asio, which has provided us with the network programming function as well as the asynchronous operations functionality to program a network application, we can now develop them easily. Since data transmission over a network can take a long time, which means acknowledgments and errors may not be available as fast as the functions that send or receive data can execute, the asynchronous operations functionality is really required in network application programming. In this book, you will learn the basics of networking and also how to develop a network application using the Boost.Asio libraries.

What this book covers

Chapter 1, Simplifying Your Network Programming in C++, explains the preparation of a C++ compiler, which will be used to compile all the source code in this book. Also, it will tell us how to compile a single source code and link to multiple source codes.

Chapter 2, Understanding the Networking Concepts, covers the network reference models, which are OSI and TCP/IP. It also provides various TCP/IP tools that we will often be using to detect whether an error has occurred in our network connection.

Chapter 3, Introducing the Boost C++ Libraries, explains how to set up the compiler in order to compile the code that contains the Boost libraries and how to build the binaries of libraries that we have to compile separately.

Chapter 4, Getting Started with Boost.Asio, talks about concurrent and nonconcurrent programming. It also discusses the I/O service, which is used to access the operating system's resources and establish communication between our program and the operating system that performs I/O requests.

Chapter 5, *Delving into the Boost.Asio Library*, walks us through how to serialize an I/O service's work in order to ensure that the order of work completely matches the order we have designed. It also covers how to handle errors and exceptions and create time delays in network programming.

Chapter 6, *Creating a Client-server Application*, discusses developing a server that is able to send and receive data traffic from a client and also how to create a client-side program to receive data traffic.

Chapter 7, *Debugging the Code and Solving the Error*, covers the debugging process to trace the errors that may be produced by an unexpected result, such as getting crash in the middle of a program execution. After reading this chapter, you will be able to solve various errors by debugging the code.

What you need for this book

To walk through this book and to successfully compile all source codes, you need a personal computer that runs Microsoft Windows 8.1 (or a later version) and contains the following software:

- MinGW-w64 for Windows, version 4.9.2
- The latest version of Notepad++
- The Boost C++ libraries, version 1.58.0

Who this book is for

This book is for C++ network programmers who have basic knowledge of network programming, but no knowledge of how to use Boost.Asio for network programming.

Conventions

In this book, you will find a number of text styles that distinguish between different kinds of information. Here are some examples of these styles and an explanation of their meaning.

Code words in text, database table names, folder names, filenames, file extensions, pathnames, dummy URLs, user input, and Twitter handles are shown as follows: "Wait for a moment until the `mingw-w64-install.exe` file is completely downloaded."

A block of code is set as follows:

```
/* rangen.cpp */
#include <cstdlib>
#include <iostream>
#include <ctime>
int main(void) {
```

When we wish to draw your attention to a particular part of a code block, the relevant lines or items are set in bold:

```
int guessNumber;
std::cout << "Select number among 0 to 10: ";
std::cin >> guessNumber;
```

Any command-line input or output is written as follows:

```
rundll32.exe sysdm.cpl,EditEnvironmentVariables
```

New terms and **important words** are shown in bold. Words that you see on the screen, for example, in menus or dialog boxes, appear in the text like this: "You will be greeted by a **Welcoming** dialog box. Just press the **Next** button to go to the **Setup Setting** dialog box."

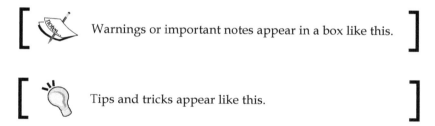

Warnings or important notes appear in a box like this.

Tips and tricks appear like this.

Reader feedback

Feedback from our readers is always welcome. Let us know what you think about this book—what you liked or disliked. Reader feedback is important for us as it helps us develop titles that you will really get the most out of.

To send us general feedback, simply e-mail feedback@packtpub.com, and mention the book's title in the subject of your message.

If there is a topic that you have expertise in and you are interested in either writing or contributing to a book, see our author guide at www.packtpub.com/authors.

Customer support

Now that you are the proud owner of a Packt book, we have a number of things to help you to get the most from your purchase.

Downloading the example code

You can download the example code files from your account at http://www. packtpub.com for all the Packt Publishing books you have purchased. If you purchased this book elsewhere, you can visit http://www.packtpub.com/support and register to have the files e-mailed directly to you.

Errata

Although we have taken every care to ensure the accuracy of our content, mistakes do happen. If you find a mistake in one of our books — maybe a mistake in the text or the code — we would be grateful if you could report this to us. By doing so, you can save other readers from frustration and help us improve subsequent versions of this book. If you find any errata, please report them by visiting http://www.packtpub. com/submit-errata, selecting your book, clicking on the **Errata Submission Form** link, and entering the details of your errata. Once your errata are verified, your submission will be accepted and the errata will be uploaded to our website or added to any list of existing errata under the Errata section of that title.

To view the previously submitted errata, go to https://www.packtpub.com/books/ content/support and enter the name of the book in the search field. The required information will appear under the **Errata** section.

Piracy

Piracy of copyrighted material on the Internet is an ongoing problem across all media. At Packt, we take the protection of our copyright and licenses very seriously. If you come across any illegal copies of our works in any form on the Internet, please provide us with the location address or website name immediately so that we can pursue a remedy.

Please contact us at copyright@packtpub.com with a link to the suspected pirated material.

We appreciate your help in protecting our authors and our ability to bring you valuable content.

Questions

If you have a problem with any aspect of this book, you can contact us at
questions@packtpub.com, and we will do our best to address the problem.

1

Simplifying Your Network Programming in C++

There are several C++ compilers that we can choose from the Web. To make it easier for you to follow all the code in this book, I have chosen a compiler that will make the programming process simpler—definitely the easiest one. In this chapter, you will discover the following topics:

- Setting up the MinGW compiler
- Compiling in C++
- Troubleshooting in GCC C++

Setting up the MinGW compiler and Text Editor

This is the hardest part—where we have to choose one compiler over the others. Even though I realize that every compiler has its own strength and weakness, I want to make it easier for you to go through all the code in this chapter. So, I suggest that you apply the same environment that we have, including the compiler that we use.

I am going to use **GCC**, the GNU Compiler Collection, because of its widely used open source. Since my environment includes Microsoft Windows as the operating system, I am going to use **Minimalistic GCC for Windows (MinGW)** as my C++ compiler. For those of you who have not heard about GCC, it is a C/C++ compiler that you can find in a Linux operating system and it is included in a Linux distribution as well. MinGW is a port of GCC to a Windows environment. Therefore, the entire code and examples in this book are applicable to any other GCC flavor.

Installing MinGW-w64

For your convenience, and since we use a 64-bit Windows operating system, we chose MinGW-w64 because it can be used for Windows 32-bits and 64-bits architecture. To install it, simply open your Internet browser and navigate to `http://sourceforge.net/projects/mingw-w64/` to go to the download page, and click on the **Download** button. Wait for a moment until the `mingw-w64-install.exe` file is completely downloaded. Refer to the following screenshot to locate the **Download** button:

Now, execute the installer file. You will be greeted by a **Welcoming** dialog box. Just press the **Next** button to go to the **Setup Setting** dialog box. In this dialog box, choose the latest GCC version (at the writing time this, it is **4.9.2**), and the rest of the options are to be chosen, as follows:

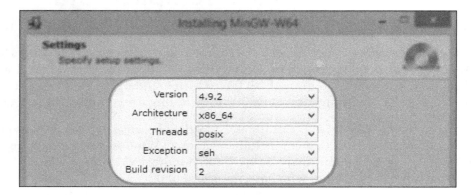

Click on the **Next** button to continue and go to the installation location option. Here, you can change the default installation location. I am going to change the installation location to C:\MinGW-w64 in order to make our next setting easier, but you can keep this default location if you want.

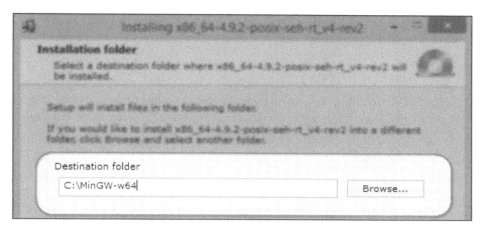

Click on the **Next** button to go to the next step and wait for a moment until the files are downloaded and the installation process is complete.

Setting up the Path environment

Now you have the C++ compiler installed on your machine, but you can only access it from its installed directory. In order to access the compiler from any directory in your system, you have to set the **PATH environment** by performing the following steps:

1. Run Command Prompt as an administrator by pressing the *Windows* + *R* key. Type cmd in the text box and, instead of pressing the *Enter* key, press *Ctrl* + *Shift* + *Enter* to run the command prompt in Administrator mode. The **User Account Control** dialog box will then appear. Choose **YES** to confirm that you intend to run Command Prompt in Administrator mode. If you do this correctly, you will get a title bar labeled **Administrator: Command Prompt**. If you do not get it, you might not have the administrator privilege. In this case, you have to contact the administrator of your computer.

2. Type the following command in Command Prompt in Administrator mode:

   ```
   rundll32.exe sysdm.cpl,EditEnvironmentVariables
   ```

3. Press the *Enter* key and the command prompt will immediately run the **Environment Variables** window. Afterwards, go to **System variables**, select the variable named **Path**, click on the **Edit** button to open the **Edit System Variable** dialog box, and then append the last **Variable value** parameter with the following string:

   ```
   ;C:\MinGW-w64\mingw64\bin
   ```

   (Otherwise, you will have to adjust the path of the installation directory if you use the default location the installation wizard is given in the previous step)

4. Click on the **OK** button on the **Edit System Variable** dialog box, and click on the **OK** button again in the **Environment Variables** dialog box to save these changes.

It is time to try our Environment Variable setting. Open a new Command Prompt window, either in Administrator or non-Administrator mode, in any active directory except `C:\MinGW-w64` and type the following command:

```
g++ --version
```

You have configured the proper settings if you see the output informing you the following:

```
g++ (x86_64-posix-seh-rev2, Built by MinGW-W64 project) 4.9.2
```

If you are showed a different version number, you might have another GCC compiler on your computer. To solve this problem, you can modify **Environment Variable** and remove all path environment settings associated with the other GCC compiler, for instance, `C:\StrawberryPerl\c\bin`.

However, if you do believe that you have followed all the steps correctly, but you still get an error message, as shown in the following snippet, you might have to restart your machine for your new system settings to be set:

```
'g++' is not recognized as an internal or external command, operable
program or batch file.
```

Choosing and installing the Text Editor

Microsoft Windows has been equipped with **Notepad**, a simple text editor to create plain text files. You can use Notepad to create a C++ file, where the file must contain only plain text formatting. You can also turn to a heavy **Integrated Development Environments** (**IDE**) when you want to edit your code, but I prefer a simple, lightweight, and extensible programming plain-text editor, so I choose to use a text editor instead of IDE. Since I will need syntax highlighting when writing code to make it easier to read and understand, I pick **Notepad++** as our text editor. You can choose your favorite text editor as long as you save the output file as plain text. Here is the sample of syntax highlighting in Notepad++:

```
C:\CPP\main.cpp - Notepad++

File  Edit  Search  View  Encoding  Language  Settings  Macro  Run  Plugins  Window  ?            X

main.cpp

  1    /* main.cpp */
  2    #include "speak.h"
  3    int main(void)
  4    {
  5        Speak speak;
  6        speak.sayHello("World");
  7        return 0;
  8    }

length : 110    lines : 8       Ln : 1   Col : 1   Sel : 0 | 0          Dos\Windows       UTF-8 w/o BOM       INS
```

If you decide to use Notepad++ as I did, you can go to `http://notepad-plus-plus.org/` to grab the latest version of Notepad++. Find the **Download** menu on the main page and select the current version link. There, you will find a link to download the installer file. Use the **Notepad++ Installer** file instead of the package file to get the easiest way to set it up on your machine by following all the instructions on the installer wizard.

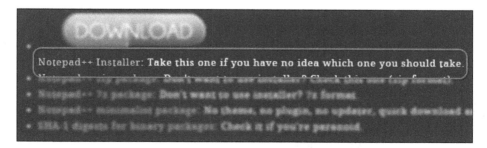

Using the GCC C++ compiler

Now that we have our development ready, we can write our first C++ program. To keep it clean, create a CPP folder in the C drive (C:\CPP) to store our sample code. You can have the same directory location on your system in order to follow all the steps more conveniently. Otherwise, you will have to make a little bit of modification if you decide to use a different directory location.

Compiling a C++ program

We won't create the Hello World! program for our first example code. It is boring in my opinion and, by now, you should already know how to code the Hello World! program. We are going to create a simple random number generator. You can use this program to play with your friends. They have to guess which number will be displayed by the program. If the answer is incorrect, you can cross out his/her face with a marker and continue playing until you are not able to recognize your friend's face anymore. Here is the code to create this generator:

```cpp
/* rangen.cpp */
#include <cstdlib>
#include <iostream>
#include <ctime>
int main(void) {
  int guessNumber;
  std::cout << "Select number among 0 to 10:";
  std::cin >> guessNumber;
  if(guessNumber < 0 || guessNumber > 10) {
    return 1;
  }
  std::srand(std::time(0));
  int randomNumber = (std::rand() % (10 + 1));
  if(guessNumber == randomNumber) {
    std::cout << "Congratulation, " <<guessNumber<<" is your
    lucky number.\n";
  }
  else {
    std::cout << "Sorry, I'm thinking about number \n" <<
    randomNumber;
  }
  return 0;
}
```

Type the code in your text editor and save it with the name of the file rangen.cpp in the C:\CPP location. Then, open Command Prompt and point the active directory to the C:\CPP location by typing the following command in Command Prompt:

cd C:\CPP

Next, type the following command in the console to compile the code:

```
g++ -Wall rangen.cpp -o rangen
```

The preceding command compiles the rangen.cpp file with an executable file named rangen.exe, which contains a bunch of machine code (the exe extension is automatically added to indicate that this file is an executable file in Microsoft Windows). The output file for the machine code is specified using the -o option. If you use this option, you have to specify the name of the output file as well; otherwise, the compiler will give you an error of a missing filename. If you omit both the -o option and the output's filename, the output is written to a default file called a.exe.

 The existing executable file that has the same name as the compiled source file in the current directory will be overwritten.

I recommend that you use the -Wall option and make it a habit since this option will turn on all the most commonly used compiler warnings. If the option is disabled, GCC will not give you any warning. Because our Random Number Generator code is completely valid, GCC will not give out any warnings while it is compiled. This is why we depend on the compiler warnings to make sure that our code is valid and is compiled cleanly.

To run the program, type rangen in the console with the C:\CPP location as the active directory, and you will be showed a welcoming word: **Select number among 0 to 10**. Do what it instructs you to and choose a number between 0 to 10. Then, press *Enter* and the program will give out a number. Compare it with your own. If both the numbers are same, you will be congratulated. However, if your chosen number is different from the number the code generated, you will be informed the same. The output of the program will look as shown in the following screenshot:

```
C:\Windows\system32\cmd.exe

c:\CPP>rangen
Select number among 0 to 10: 3
Sorry, I'm thinking about number 1

c:\CPP>rangen
Select number among 0 to 10: 6
Sorry, I'm thinking about number 4

c:\CPP>rangen
Select number among 0 to 10: 10
Sorry, I'm thinking about number 7

c:\CPP>
```

Unfortunately, I never guessed the correct number in the three times that I tried. Indeed, it is not easy to guess which number the `rand()` function has generated, even if you use a new seed every time the number is generated. In order to minimize confusion, I am going to dissect the `rangen.cpp` code, as follows:

```
int guessNumber;
std::cout << "Select number among 0 to 10: ";
std::cin >> guessNumber;
```

I reserved a variable called `guessNumber` to store the integer number from the user and used the `std::cin` command to obtain the number that was input from the console.

```
if(guessNumber < 0 || guessNumber > 10) {
    return 1;
}
```

If the user gives an out-of-range number, notify the operating system that there is an error that has occurred in the program—I sent Error 1, but in practice, you can send any number—and let it take care of the error.

```
std::srand(std::time(0));
int randomNumber = (std::rand() % (10 + 1);
```

The `std::srand` function is used to initialize the seed, and in order to generate a different random number every time the `std::rand()` function is invoked, we use the `std::time(0)` function from the header `ctime`. To generate a range of random numbers, we use the `modulo` method that will generate a random number from 0 to (n-1) if you invoke a function like `std::rand() % n`. If you want to include the number *n* as well, simply add *n* with 1.

```
if(guessNumber == randomNumber) {
    std::cout << "Congratulation ,"<< guessNumber<<" is your
    lucky number.\n";
}
else {
    std::cout << "Sorry, I'm thinking about number " <<
    randomNumber << "\n";
}
```

Here is the fun part, the program compares the user's guessed number with the generated random number. Whatever happens, the user will be informed of the result by the program. Let's take a look at the following code:

```
return 0;
```

A 0 return tells the operating system that the program has been terminated normally and that there is no need to worry about it. Let's take a look at the following code:

```
#include <cstdlib>
#include <iostream>
#include <ctime>
```

Do not forget to include the first three headers in the preceding code since they contain the function that we used in this program, such as the `time()` function is defined in the `<ctime>` header, the `srand()` function and the `rand()` function are defined in the `<cstdlib>` header, and the `cout()` and `cin()` functions are defined in the `<iostream>` header.

If you find that it is hard to guess a number that the program has generated, this is because we use the current time as the random generator seed, and the consequence of this is that the generated number will always be different in every invocation of the program. Here is the screenshot of when I could guess the generated random number correctly after about six to seven attempts (for all the program invocations, we guessed the number incorrectly except for the last attempt):

Compiling multiple source files

Sometimes, we have to modify our code when it has bugs or errors. If we just make a single file that contains all the lines of code, we will be confused when we want to modify the source or it will be hard for us to understand the flow of the program. To solve the problem, we can split up our code into multiple files where every file contains only two to three functions so that it is easy to understand and maintain them.

We have already been able to generate random numbers, so now, let's take a look at the password generator program. We are going to use it to try compiling multiple source files. I will create three files to demonstrate how to compile multiple source files, which are pwgen_fn.h, pwgen_fn.cpp, and passgen.cpp. We will start from the pwgen_fn.h file whose code is as follows:

```
/* pwgen_fn.h */
#include <string>
#include <cstdlib>
#include <ctime>
class PasswordGenerator {
  public:
    std::string Generate(int);
};
```

The preceding code is used to declare the class name. In this example, the class name is PasswordGenerator, and what it will do in this case is generate the password while the implementation is stored in the .cpp file. The following is a listing of the pwgen_fn.cpp file, which contains the implementation of the Generate() function:

```
/* pwgen_fn.cpp */
#include "pwgen_fn.h"
std::string PasswordGenerator::Generate(int passwordLength) {
  int randomNumber;
  std::string password;
  std::srand(std::time(0));
  for(int i=0; i < passwordLength; i++) {
    randomNumber = std::rand() % 94 + 33;
    password += (char) randomNumber;
  }
  return password;
}
```

The main entry file, `passgen.cpp`, contains a program that uses the `PasswordGenerator` class:

```cpp
/* passgen.cpp */
#include <iostream>
#include "pwgen_fn.h"
int main(void) {
  int passLen;
  std::cout << "Define password length: ";
  std::cin >> passLen;
  PasswordGenerator pg;
  std::string password = pg.Generate(passLen);
  std::cout << "Your password: "<< password << "\n";
  return 0;
}
```

From the preceding three source files, we will produce a single executable file. To do so, go to Command Prompt and type the following command in it:

```
g++ -Wall passgen.cpp pwgen_fn.cpp -o passgen
```

I did not get any warning or error, so even you should not. The preceding command compiles the `passgen.cpp` and `pwgen_fn.cpp` files and then links them together to a single executable file named `passgen.exe`. The `pwgen_fn.h` file, since it is the header file that has same name as the source file, does not need to state the same in the command.

Here is what you will get if you run the program by typing the `passgen` command in the console window; you will get a different password every time the program is run:

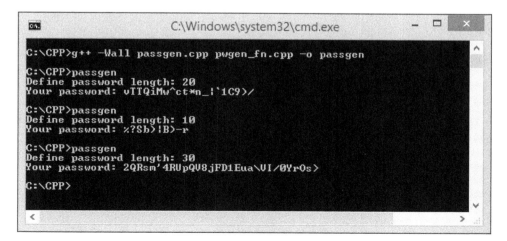

Now, it is time for us to dissect the preceding source code. We will start from the pwgen_fn.h file, which only contains the function declaration, as follows:

```
std::string Generate(int);
```

As you can see from the declaration, the Generate() function will have a parameter with the int type and will return the std::string function. We do not define a name for the parameter in the header file since it will be matched with the source file automatically.

Open the pwgen_fn.cpp file, to see the following statement:

```
std::string PasswordGenerator::Generate(int passwordLength)
```

Here, we can specify the parameter name, which is passwordLength. In this case, we can have two or more functions with the same name as long as they are in different classes. Let's take a look at the following code:

```
int randomNumber;
std::string password;
```

I reserved the variable named randomNumber to store random numbers generated by the rand() function and the password parameter to store the ASCII converted from the random number. Let's take a look at the following code:

```
std::srand(std::time(0));
```

The seed random srand() function is the same as what we used in our previous code to generate a random seed. We used it in order to produce a different number every time the rand() function is invoked. Let's take a look at the following code:

```
for(int i=0; i < passwordLength; i++) {
  randomNumber = std::rand() % 94 + 33;
  password += (char) randomNumber;
}
return password;
```

The for iteration depends on the passwordLength parameter that the user has defined. With the random number generator statement std::rand() % 94 + 33, we can generate the number that represents the ASCII printable character based on its code from 33 to 126. For more detailed information about the ASCII code table, you can go to http://en.wikipedia.org/wiki/ASCII. Let's take a look at the following code:

```
#include "pwgen_fn.h"
```

The #include header's single line will call all headers included in the pwgen_fn.h file, so we do not need to declare the included header in this source file as follows:

```
#include <string>
#include <cstdlib>
#include <ctime>
```

Now, we move to our main entry code, which is stored in the passgen.cpp file:

```
int passLen;
std::cout << "Define password length: ";
std::cin >> passLen;
```

First, the user decides how long a password he/she wants to have, and the program stores it in the passLen variable:

```
PasswordGenerator pg;
std::string password = pg.Generate(passLen);
std::cout << "Your password: "<< password << "\n";
```

Then, the program instantiates the PasswordGenerator class and invokes the Generate() function to produce a password with the length that the user has defined before.

If you look at the passgen.cpp file again, you will find that there is a difference between the two forms of the include statement #include <iostream> (with angle brackets) and #include "pwgen_fn.h" (with quotation marks). By using angle brackets in the #include header statement, the compiler will look for the system header file directories, but does not look inside the current directory by default. With the quotation marks in the #include header statement, the compiler will search for the header files in the current directory before looking in the system header file directories.

Compiling and linking a program separately

We can split up a large program into a set of source files and compile them separately. Suppose we have many tiny files and we just want to edit a single line in one of the files, it will be very time consuming if we compile all the files while we just need to modify a single file.

By using the -c option, we can compile the individual source code to produce an object file that has the .o extension. In this first stage, a file is compiled without creating an executable file. Then, in the second stage, the object files are linked together by a separate program called the linker. The linker combines all the object files together to create a single executable file. Using the previous passgen.cpp, pwgen_fn.cpp, and pwgen_fn.h source files, we will try to create two object files and then link them together to produce a single executable file. Use the following two commands to do the same:

```
g++ -Wall -c passgen.cpp pwgen_fn.cpp
g++ -Wall passgen.o pwgen_fn.o -o passgen
```

The first command, using the -c option, will create two object files that have the same name as the source file name, but with different extensions. The second command will link them together and produce the output executable file that has the name stated after the -o option, which is the passgen.exe file.

In case you need to edit the passgen.cpp file without touching the two other files, you just require to compile the passgen.cpp file, as follows:

```
g++ -Wall -c passgen.cpp
```

Then, you need to run the linking command like the preceding second command.

Detecting a warning in the C++ program

As we discussed previously, a compiler warning is an essential aid to be sure of the code's validity. Now, we will try to find the error from the code that we created. Here is a C++ code that contains an uninitialized variable, which will give us an unpredictable result:

```cpp
/* warning.cpp */
#include <iostream>
#include <string>
int main (void) {
  std::string name;
  int age;
  std::cout << "Hi " << name << ", your age is " << age << "\n";
}
```

Then, we will run the following command to compile the preceding `warning.cpp` code:

```
g++ -Wall -c warning.cpp
```

Sometimes, we are unable to detect this error since it is not obvious at the first sight. However, by enabling the `-Wall` option, we can prevent the error because if we compile the preceding code with the warning option enabled, the compiler will produce a warning message, as shown in the following code:

```
warning.cpp: In function 'int main()':
warning.cpp:7:52: warning: 'age' may be used uninitialized in this
function [-Wmaybe-uninitialized]
std::cout << "Hi " << name << ", your age is " << age << "\n";]
```

The warning message says that the `age` variable is not initialized in the `warning.cpp` file on the line 7, column 52. The messages produced by GCC always have the **file:line-number:column-number:error-type:message** form. The error type distinguishes between the error messages, which prevent the successful compilation, and warning messages, which indicate the possible problems (but do not stop the program from compiling).

Clearly, it is very dangerous to develop a program without checking for compiler warnings. If there are any functions that are not used correctly, they can cause the program to crash or produce incorrect results. After turning the compiler warning option on, the `-Wall` option catches many of the common errors that occur in C++ programming.

Knowing other important options in the GCC C++ compiler

GCC supports **ISO C++ 1998**, **C++ 2003**, and also **C++ 2011** standard in version 4.9.2. Selecting this standard in GCC is done using one of these options: `-ansi`, `-std=c++98`, `-std=c++03`, or `-std=c++11`. Let's look at the following code and give it the name `hash.cpp`:

```
/* hash.cpp */
#include <iostream>
#include <functional>
#include <string>
int main(void) {
  std::string plainText = "";
```

```
    std::cout << "Input string and hit Enter if ready: ";
    std::cin >> plainText;
    std::hash<std::string> hashFunc;
    size_t hashText = hashFunc(plainText);
    std::cout << "Hashing: " << hashText << "\n";
    return 0;
}
```

If you compile and run the program, it will give you a hash number for every plain text user input. However, it is little tricky to compile the preceding code. We have to define which ISO standard we want to use. Let's take a look at the following five compilation commands and try them one by one in our Command Prompt window:

```
g++ -Wall hash.cpp -o hash

g++ -Wall -ansi hash.cpp -o hash

g++ -Wall -std=c++98 hash.cpp -o hash

g++ -Wall -std=c++03 hash.cpp -o hash

g++ -Wall -std=c++11 hash.cpp -o hash
```

When we run the first four preceding compilation commands, we should get the following error message:

```
hash.cpp: In function 'int main()':
hash.cpp:10:2: error: 'hash' is not a member of 'std'
   std::hash<std::string> hashFunc;
hash.cpp:10:23: error: expected primary-expression before '>' token
   std::hash<std::string> hashFunc;
hash.cpp:10:25: error: 'hashFunc' was not declared in this scope
   std::hash<std::string> hashFunc;
```

It says that there is no hash in the std class. Actually, this is not true as a hash has been defined in the header <string> since C++ 2011. To solve this problem, we can run the last preceding compilation command, and if it does not throw an error anymore, then we can run the program by typing hash in the console window.

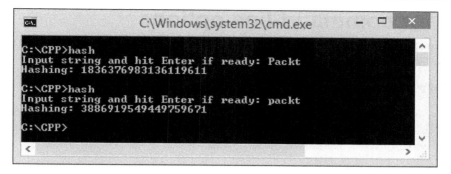

As you can see in the preceding screenshot, I invoked the program twice and gave **Packt** and **packt** as the input. Although I just changed a character, the entire hash changed dramatically. This is why hashing is used to detect any change in data or a file if they are transferred, just to make sure the data is not altered.

For more information about ISO C++11 features available in GCC, go to `http://gcc.gnu.org/projects/cxx0x.html`. To obtain all the diagnostics required by the standard, you should also specify the `-pedantic` option (or the `-pedantic-errors` option if you want to handle warnings as errors).

The `-ansi` option alone does not cause non-ISO programs to be rejected gratuitously. For that, the `-pedantic` option or the `-pedantic-errors` option is required in addition with the `-ansi` option.

Troubleshooting in the GCC C++ compiler

GCC provides several help and diagnostic options to assist in troubleshooting problems with the compilation process. The options that you can use to ease your troubleshooting process are explained in the upcoming sections.

Help for command-line options

Use the `help` options to get a summary of the top-level GCC command-line options. The command for this is as follows:

```
g++ --help
```

To display a complete list of the options for GCC and its associated programs, such as the GNU Linker and GNU Assembler, use the preceding `help` option with the verbose (`-v`) option:

```
g++ -v --help
```

The complete list of options produced by the preceding command is extremely long—you may wish to go through it using the `more` command or redirect the output to a file for reference, as follows:

```
g++ -v --help 2>&1 | more
```

Version numbers

You can find the version number of your installed GCC installation using the `version` option, as shown in the following command:

```
g++ --version
```

In my system, if I run the preceding command, I will get an output like this:

```
g++ (x86_64-posix-seh-rev2, Built by MinGW-W64 project) 4.9.2
```

This depends on your setting that you adjust at the installation process.

The version number is important when investigating compilation problems, since older versions of GCC may be missing some features that a program uses. The version number has the `major-version.minor-version` or `major-version.minor-version.micro-version` form, where the additional third "micro" version number (as shown in the preceding command) is used for subsequent bug fix releases in a release series.

The verbose compilation

The -v option can also be used to display detailed information about the exact sequence of commands that are used to compile and link a program. Here is an example that shows you the verbose compilation of the hello.cpp program:

```
g++ -v -Wall rangen.cpp
```

After this, you will get something like this in the console:

```
Using built-in specs.
COLLECT_GCC=g++
COLLECT_LTO_WRAPPER=C:/mingw-w64/bin/../libexec/gcc/x86_64-w64-
mingw32/4.9.2/lto-wrapper.exe
Target: x86_64-w64-mingw32
Configured with: ../../../src/gcc-4.9.2/configure -
...Thread model: posix
gcc version 4.9.2 (x86_64-posix-seh-rev2, Built by MinGW-W64 project)
...
```

The output produced by the -v option can be useful whenever there is a problem with the compilation process itself. It displays the full directory paths used to search for header files and libraries, the predefined preprocessor symbols, and the object files and libraries used for linking.

Summary

We successfully prepared the C++ compiler and you learned how to compile the source code file you created using the compiler. Do not forget to use the -Wall (Warning All) option every time you compile the source code because it is important to avoid a warning and subtle error. Also, it is important to use the -ansi and -pedantic options so that your source code is able to be compiled in any compiler, as it will check the ANSI standard and reject non-ISO programs.

Now, we can go to the next chapter to learn the networking concept so that you can understand network architecture in order to ease your network application programming process.

2
Understanding the Networking Concepts

Before we start coding a network application, it is better for us to understand how a network works. In this chapter, we will dig up network concepts with their contents. The topics that we'll cover in this chapter are as follows:

- Distinguishing between the OSI model and the TCP/IP model
- Exploring IP addresses in both IPv4 and IPv6
- Troubleshooting TCP/IP problems using various tools

An introduction to networking systems

Network architecture is structured with layers and protocols. Each **layer** in the architecture has its own role, while its main purpose is to offer a certain service to the higher layer and communicate with the adjoining layers. However, a **protocol** is a collection of rules and conventions that are used by all the communicating parties to standardize the communication process. For instance, when the layer n in a device communicates with another layer n in another device, for the communication to take place, they have to use the same protocol.

There are two popular network architectures that are used nowadays: the **Open Systems Interconnection** (**OSI**) and **TCP/IP** reference models. We will dig deeper to understand each reference model with its advantages and disadvantages so that we can decide which model should be used in our network application.

The OSI reference model

The OSI model is used to connect to the open systems — these are the systems that are open and communicate with other systems. By using this model, we do not depend on an operating system anymore, so we are allowed to communicate with any operating system on any computer. This model contains seven layers, where each layer has a specific function and defines the way data is handled on certain different layers. The seven layers that are contained in this model are the **Physical layer**, **Data Link layer**, **Network layer**, **Transport layer**, **Session layer**, **Presentation layer**, and the **Application layer**.

The Physical layer

This is the first layer in the OSI model and contains a definition of the network's physical specification, including the physical media (cables and connectors) and basic devices (repeaters and hubs). The layer is responsible for the input raw bits transmission data stream into zeros and for the ones that are on the communication channel. It then places the data onto the physical media. It is concerned with data transmission integrity and makes sure that the bits that are sent from one device are exactly the same as the data that is received by the other device.

The Data Link layer

The main role of the Data Link layer is to provide a link for raw data transmission. Before the data is transmitted, it is broken up into data frames, and the Data Link layer transmits them consecutively. The receiver will send back an *acknowledge frame* for each frame that has been sent if the service is reliable.

This layer consists of two sublayers: **Logical Link Control** (**LLC**) and **Media Access Control** (**MAC**). The LLC sublayer is responsible for transmission error checking and deals with frame transmission, while the MAC sublayer defines how to retrieve data from the physical media or store data in the physical media.

We can also find the MAC address, also called as the **physical address**, in this layer. The MAC address is used to identify every device that connects to the network because it is unique for each device. Using Command Prompt, we can obtain the address by typing the following command in the console window:

```
ipconfig /all
```

We will get the console output, as follows, after ignoring all other information except **Windows IP Configuration** and **Wireless LAN adapter Wi-Fi**. We can find the MAC address in the **Physical Address** section, which is **80-19-34-CB-BF-FB** for my own environment. You will get a different result since the MAC address is unique for every device:

```
Windows IP Configuration

    Host Name . . . . . . . . . . . . : HOST1
    Primary Dns Suffix  . . . . . . . :
    Node Type . . . . . . . . . . . . : Hybrid
    IP Routing Enabled. . . . . . . . : No
    WINS Proxy Enabled. . . . . . . . : No


Wireless LAN adapter Wi-Fi:
    Connection-specific DNS Suffix  . :
    Description . . . . . . . . . . . : Intel(R) Wireless-N 7260
    Physical Address. . . . . . . . . : 80-19-34-CB-BF-FB
    DHCP Enabled. . . . . . . . . . . : Yes
    Autoconfiguration Enabled . . . . : Yes
    Link-local IPv6 Address . . . . . : fe80::f14e:d5e6:aa0a:5855%3
    (Preferred)
    IPv4 Address. . . . . . . . . . . : 192.168.1.4(Preferred)
    Subnet Mask . . . . . . . . . . . : 255.255.255.0
    Default Gateway . . . . . . . . . : 192.168.1.254
    DHCP Server . . . . . . . . . . . : 192.168.1.254
    DHCPv6 IAID . . . . . . . . . . . : 58726708
    DHCPv6 Client DUID. . . . . . . . : 00-01-00-01-1C-89-E6-3E-68-F7-
    28-1E-61-66
    DNS Servers . . . . . . . . . . . : 192.168.1.254
    NetBIOS over Tcpip. . . . . . . . : Enabled
```

The MAC address contains twelve hexadecimal characters, where two digits are paired with each other. The first six digits represent the **organizationally unique identifier** and the remaining digits represent the **manufacturer serial number**. If you are really curious to know what this number means, you can go to www.macvendorlookup.com and fill the text box with our MAC address to know more about it. In my own system, I got Intel Corporate as the vendor company name, which is the same as the brand of my installed network card.

The Network layer

The Network layer is responsible for defining the best way to route the packets from a source to the destination device. It will generate routing tables using **Internet Protocol (IP)** as the routing protocol, and the IP address is used to make sure that the data gets its route to the required destination. There are two versions of IP nowadays: **IPv4** and **IPv6**. In IPv4, we use 32-bit addresses to address the protocol and we use 128-bit addresses in IPv6. You are going to learn more about Internet Protocol, IPv4, and IPv6 in the next topic.

The Transport layer

The Transport layer is responsible for transferring data from a source to destination. It will split up the data into smaller parts, or in this case **segments**, and then will join all the segments to restore the data to its initial form in the destination.

There are two main protocols that work in this layer: the **Transmission Control Protocol (TCP)** and the **User Datagram Protocol (UDP)**. TCP supplies the delivery of data by establishing a session. The data will not be transmitted until a session is established. TCP is also known as the **connection-oriented protocol**, which means that the session has to be established before transmitting the data. UDP is a method of delivering data with the best efforts, but does not give a guaranteed delivery because it does not establish a session. Therefore, UDP is also known as the **connection-less protocol**. In-depth explanation about TCP and UDP can be found in the next topic.

The Session layer

The Session layer is responsible for the establishment, maintenance, and termination of the session. We can analogize the session like a connection between two devices on the network. For example, if we want to send a file from a computer to another, this layer will establish the connection first before the file can be sent. This layer will then make sure that the connection is still up until the file is sent completely. Finally, this layer will terminate the connection if it is no longer needed. The connection we talk about is the session.

This layer also makes sure that the data from a different application is not interchanged. For example, if we run the Internet browser, chat application, and download manager at the same time, this layer will be responsible for establishing the session for every single application and ensure that they remain separated from other applications.

There are three communication methods that are used by this layer: the **simplex**, **half-duplex**, or **full-duplex** method. In the simplex method, data can only be transferred by one party, so the other cannot transfer any data. This method is no longer common in use, since we need applications that can interact with each other. In the half-duplex method, any data can be transferred to all the involved devices, but only one device can transfer the data in the time, after it completes the sending process. Then, the others can also send and transfer data. The full-duplex method can transfer data to all the devices at the same time. To send and receive data, this method uses different paths.

The Presentation layer

The Presentation layer role is used to determine the data that has been sent, to translate the data into the appropriate format, and then to present it. For example, we send an MP3 file over the network and the file is split up into several segments. Then, using the header information on the segment, this layer will construct the file by translating the segments.

Moreover, this layer is responsible for data compression and decompression because all the data transmitted over the Internet is compressed to save the bandwidth. This layer is also responsible for data encryption and decryption in order to secure communication between two devices.

The Application layer

The Application layer deals with the computer application that is used by a user. Only the application that connects to a network will connect to this layer. This layer contains several protocols that are needed by a user, which are as follows:

- **The Domain Name System (DNS)**: This protocol is the one that finds the hostname of an IP address. With this system, we do not need to memorize every IP address any longer, just the hostname. We can easily remember a word in the hostname instead of a bunch of numbers in the IP address.

- **The Hypertext Transfer Protocol (HTTP)**: This protocol is the one that transmits data over the Internet on web pages. We also have the HTTPS format that is used to send encrypted data for security issues.

- **The File Transfer Protocol (FTP)**: This protocol is the one that is used to transfer files from or to an FTP server.

- **The Trivial FTP (TFTP)**: This protocol is similar to FTP, which is used to send smaller files.

- **The Dynamic Host Configuration Protocol (DHCP)**: This protocol is a method that is used to assign the TCP/IP configuration dynamically.

- **The Post Office Protocol (POP3)**: This protocol is an electronic mail protocol used to get back e-mails from POP3 servers. The server is usually hosted by an **Internet Service Provider (ISP)**.

- **The Simple Mail Transfer Protocol (SMTP)**: This protocol is in contrast with POP3 and is used to send electronic mails.

- **The Internet Message Access Protocol (IMAP)**: This protocol is used to receive e-mail messages. With this protocol, users can save their e-mail messages on their folder on a local computer.

- **The Simple Network Management Protocol (SNMP)**: This protocol is used to manage network devices (routers and switches) and detect problems to report them before they become significant.

- **The Server Message Block (SMB)**: This protocol is an FTP that is used on Microsoft networks primarily for file and printer sharing.

This layer also decides whether enough network resources are available for network access. For instance, if you want to surf the Internet using an Internet browser, the Application layer decides whether access to the Internet is available using HTTP.

Let's see the following figure to see which all protocols are included in the OSI layer:

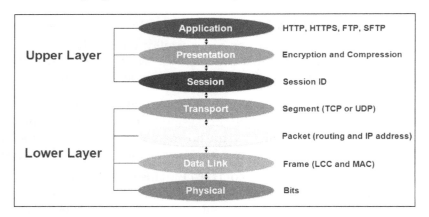

We can divide all the seven layers into two section layers: the **Upper Layer** and **Lower Layer**. The upper layer is responsible for interacting with the user and is less concerned about the low-level details, whereas the lower layer is responsible for transferring data over the network, such as formatting and encoding.

The format of data traveling is different for each layer. There are bits for the Physical layer, frame for the Data Link layer, and so on.

The TCP/IP reference model

The TCP/IP model was created before the OSI model. This model works in a similar way to the OSI model, except that it just contains four layers. Each layer on the TCP/IP model corresponds to the layers of the OSI model. The TCP/IP Application layer maps the 5, 6, and 7 layers of the OSI model. The TCP/IP Transport layer maps the layer 4 of the OSI model. The TCP/IP Internet layer maps the layer 3 of the OSI model. The TCP/IP Link layer maps the layers 1 and 2 of the OSI model. Let's see the following figure for further details:

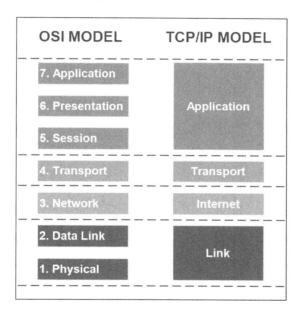

These are the main roles of each layer in the TCP/IP model:

- The Link layer is responsible for determining the protocols and physical devices that are used in the data transmission process.
- The Internet layer is responsible for determining the best routing for the data transmission process by addressing the packet.
- The Transport layer is responsible for establishing the communication between the two devices and sending the packet.
- The Application layer is responsible for providing services to applications that run on a computer. Because of the absence of the session and presentation layers, applications have to be included in any required session and presentation functions.

Here are the protocols and devices that are involved in the TCP/IP model:

Layer	Protocol	Device
Application	HTTP, HTTPS, SMTP, POP3, and DNS	Proxy Server and Firewall
Transport	TCP and UDP	-
Internet	IP and ICMP	Router
Link	Ethernet, Token Ring, and Frame Relay	Hub, Modem, and Repeater

Understanding TCP and UDP

As we discussed earlier in this chapter in the *Transport layer* section, TCP and UDP are the main protocols that are used to transfer data across a network. The delivery mechanisms that they have are different from each other. TCP has acknowledgments, sequence numbers, and flow control in transferring data process to provide a guaranteed delivery, whereas UDP does not provide a guaranteed delivery but provides a delivery with best efforts.

Transmission Control Protocol

TCP performs a three-way handshaking process before the protocol establishes the session. This is done in order to provide a guaranteed delivery. Refer to the following figure to understand the three-way handshaking process:

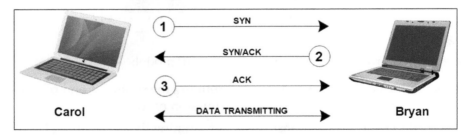

From the preceding image, imagine that Carol's device wants to transfer data to Bryan's device and that they need to perform a three-way handshaking process. First, Carol's device sends a packet to Bryan's device with the **synchronize (SYN)** flag enabled. Once Bryan's device receives the packet, it replies with sending another packet that has both the SYN and **acknowledge (ACK)** flags enabled. Lastly, Carol's device completes the handshaking process by sending a third packet with the ACK flag enabled. Now, both devices have an established session and an assurance that the other device is working. The data transmission is then ready to take place after the session is established.

In the security area, we know the term "SYN-Flood", which is a denial-of-service attack, where an attacker sends a succession of SYN requests to a target's system in an attempt to consume enough server resources to make the system unresponsive to legitimate traffic. The attacker just sends SYN without sending the expected ACK, causing the server to send the SYN-ACK to a falsified IP address — which will not send an ACK because it "knows" that it never sent the SYN.

TCP also splits up the data into smaller segments and uses sequence numbers to track these segments. Each separated segment is assigned different sequence numbers, such as 1 to 20. The destination device then receives each segment and uses the sequence numbers to reassemble the file based on the order of the sequence.

For instance, consider that Carol wants to download a JPEG image file from Bryan's device. After establishing the session in a three-way handshaking process, the two devices determine how big the single segment is and how many segments need to be sent between acknowledgments. The total number of segments that can be sent at a time is known as the TCP **sliding window**. The data in the segment is not valid anymore if a single bit is broken or lost in transmission. TCP uses **Cyclical Redundancy Check** (**CRC**) to identify the broken or lost data by verifying that the data is intact in each segment. If there is any corrupt or missing segment in transmission, Carol's device will send a **negative acknowledge** (**NACK**) packet and then will request the corrupt or missing segment; otherwise, Carol's device will send an ACK packet and request the next segment.

User Datagram Protocol

UDP does not perform any handshaking process before sending data. It just sends the data directly to the destination device; however, it puts in its best effort to forward the messages. Imagine that we are waiting to receive a message from our friend. We call his/her phone to receive our message. If our call is not answered, we can send the e-mail or text message to inform our friend. If our friend does not reply to our e-mail or text messages, we can send regular e-mails. However, all techniques that we talked about do not give any assurance that our message was received. But still, we make our best efforts to forward the message until this works. This our best effort in analogy of sending e-mails is similar with best-effort term for UDP. It will give its best effort to ensure that the data is received by the receiver, even though there is no assurance that the data was received.

So, why is UDP used even though it is not reliable? Sometimes we need a communication which has fast speed data transfer even though has a little bit data corruption. For instance, streaming audio, streaming video, and **Voice over IP (VoIP)** use UDP to make sure that they have fast speed data transfer. Although the UDP must have had lost packets, we are still able to get all the messages clearly.

However, although UDP does not check the connection before transmitting data, it actually uses a checksum to validate the data. The checksum can check whether the received data is altered or not by comparing the checksum value.

Understanding ports

In computer networking, a **port** is an endpoint to send or receive data. A port is recognized by its **port number**, which contains a 16-bit number. The logical port number is used by both TCP and UDP to trace the contents of a packet and helps TCP/IP obtain the packet of the application or service that will process the data when it is received by the device.

There are a total of 65536 TCP ports and 65536 UDP ports. We can divide the TCP ports into three port ranges, which are:

- Well-known ports from 0 to 1023 are ports that have been registered by the **Internet Assigned Numbers Authority (IANA)** to associate with specific protocols or applications.

- Registered ports from 1024 to 49151 are ports that have been registered by IANA for a specific protocol, but unused ports in this range can be assigned by computer applications.

- Dynamic ports from 49152 to 65535 are unregistered ports and can be assigned for any purpose.

 To get more details about all the ports in TCP and UDP, we can go to en.wikipedia.org/wiki/List_of_TCP_and_UDP_port_numbers. Also, to know about all the assigned ports that have been registered by IANA, go to www.iana.org/assignments/port-numbers.

To understand the port concept, consider that we have an e-mail client installed in our computer, such as Thunderbird or Microsoft Outlook. Now, we want to send an e-mail to the Gmail server and then grab all the incoming e-mails from the server to save them on our local computer. The steps to send an e-mail are as follows:

1. Our computer assigns a random unused port number, such as 48127, to send the e-mail to the Gmail SMTP server to the port 25.

2. When the e-mail arrives at the SMTP server, it recognizes that the data has come from the port 25 and then forwards the data to the SMTP, which handles the service.

3. Once the e-mail is received, the server sends the acknowledgement to the port 48127 in our computer to inform the computer that the e-mail has been received.

4. After our computer completely receives the acknowledgement from the port 48127, it sends an e-mail to the e-mail client, and the e-mail client then moves the e-mail from Outbox to the Sent folder.

Similar to the steps for sending an e-mail, to receive an e-mail, we have to deal with a port. The steps for which are as follows:

1. Our computer assigns a random unused port number, such as 48128, to send a request to the Gmail POP3 server to the port 110.

2. When the e-mail arrives at the POP3 server, it recognizes that the data has come from the port 110 and then forwards the data to POP3, which handles the service.

3. The POP3 server then sends an e-mail to our computer on the port 48128.

4. After our computer receives the e-mail from the port 48128, it sends the e-mail to our e-mail client and then moves it to the Inbox folder. It also automatically saves the mail to the local computer.

Exploring the Internet Protocol

IP is a primary communication protocol that is used to deliver a datagram across networks. The datagram itself is a transfer unit associated with a packet-switched network. The role of IP is to deliver packets from the host to the host based on the IP address, which is stated in the packet's header. There are two versions of IP that are commonly used nowadays, which are IPv4 and IPv6.

Internet Protocol Version 4 – IPv4

IPv4 has become the standard IP address since 1980s and is used to obtain TCP/IP traffic from a computer to another over the network. An IP address is unique for every device connected over the Internet, and all devices can communicate with each other over the Internet as long as they have a valid IP address.

A valid IP address is constructed by four decimal numbers that are separated by three dots. The address only contains a decimal number from 0 to 255. We can say that 10.161.4.25 is a valid IP address since it contains four decimal numbers between 0 to 255 and is separated by three dots, while 192.2.256.4 is an invalid IP address because it contains decimal numbers greater than 255.

The decimal numbers actually convert the result from 8 binary digits. So, for the maximum 8-bit number, we will have 1111 1111 or 255 in decimal. This is why the range of a decimal number in an IP address is from 0 (0000 0000) to 255 (1111 1111).

To know our IP address configuration, we can use the ipconfig /all command again in our Command Prompt window. Then, it will display the output as follows:

```
Wireless LAN adapter Wi-Fi:
    Connection-specific DNS Suffix  . :
    Link-local IPv6 Address . . . . . : fe80::f14e:d5e6:aa0a:5855%3
    IPv4 Address. . . . . . . . . . . : 10.1.6.165
    Subnet Mask . . . . . . . . . . . : 255.255.255.0
    Default Gateway . . . . . . . . . : 10.1.6.1
```

The output will show the IP address in the IPv4 address and the IPv6 address. We can also see that in my device, 10.1.6.1 is used as a default gateway of the system. The Default Gateway parameter is a point on the computer network that is used to provide a path for the unmatched IP address or subnets.

An IP address must contain these two components: a **network ID** to identify the subnetwork or subnet where the computer is located and a **host ID** to identify the computer within that subnet. Every network ID indicates a group of hosts on a subnet of a network. Devices that have the same network IDs must have unique host IDs. If two or more devices have the same host ID and the same network ID (the IP address is the same for all four decimal numbers), there will be an IP address conflict.

For local networks, the **subnet mask** is used to identify the portion of a network ID and a host ID in the IP address. The following are a few common subnet masks:

- 255.0.0.0
- 255.255.0.0
- 255.255.255.0

Imagine that we have the IP address 190.23.4.51 and the subnet mask 255.255.0.0. Now, we can find the network ID using the Boolean AND logic for each bit of the IP address corresponding to the subnet mask. The following table will convert the IP address and subnet mask into a binary digit and then use the Boolean AND logic to find out the network ID:

	1st Octet	2nd Octet	3rd Octet	4th Octet
190.23.4.51	1011 1110	0001 0111	0000 0100	0011 0011
255.255.0.0	1111 1111	1111 1111	0000 0000	0000 0000
Network ID:	1011 1110	0001 0111	0000 0000	0000 0000

From the preceding table, we can obtain the network ID, which is 190.23.0.0.

The adjacent maximum number has to be applied in a subnet mask. This means that if the first zero is decided to be used, the remaining numbers have to be zero. So, a subnet mask of 255.0.255.0 is invalid. A subnet mask is also not allowed to begin with zero. This means that a subnet mask of 0.255.0.0 is invalid as well.

IPv4 can be classified into three primary address classes: Class A, Class B, and Class C. The class of the address is defined by the first number in the IP address and the subnet mask is predefined for each class. Here are the three ranges for each class:

Class	The first number	Range of the IP address	Subnet mask
Class A	1 to 126	1.0.0.0 to 126.255.255.254	255.0.0.0
Class B	128 to 191	128.0.0.0 to 191.255.255.254	255.255.0.0
Class C	192 to 223	192.0.0.0 to 223.255.255.254	255.255.255.0

Our computer is able to determine the class of the IP address by just looking at the first two bits after converting the first decimal number in the IP address. For instance, in Class A with the range 1 to 126, the binary digit is between 0000 0001 to 0111 1110. The first two bits might be 0 and 0 or 0 and 1. Class B with the range from 128 to 191 has the range in binary digits from 1000 0000 to 1011 1111. This means that the highest first bit is always 1 and the second is always 0. Class C with the range from 192 to 223 has the range in binary digits from 1100 0000 to 1101 1111. The bits will be all 1 for the first two bits. Refer to the following table to conclude how a computer determines the class of an IP address by just checking the first two bits of the IP address (here, X is ignored and can be any hexadecimal character):

Class	First number in binary digits
Class A	00XXXXXX
	01XXXXXX
Class B	10XXXXXX
Class C	11XXXXXX

By classifying the IP address, we can also determine the subnet mask by just looking at the IP address because each class has a different subnet mask, shown as follows:

Class	Range	Subnet Mask
Class A addresses	0 -126	255.0.0.0
Class B addresses	128 to 191	255.255.0.0
Class C addresses	192 to 223	255.255.255.0

By knowing the subnet mask, we can easily know the network ID. Suppose that we have these three IP addresses:

- 174.12.1.8
- 192.168.1.15
- 10.70.4.13

Now, we can determine the network ID as follows:

The IP address	Class	Subnet mask	The Network ID
174.12.1.8	Class B	255.255.0.0	174.12.0.0
192.168.1.15	Class C	255.255.255.0	192.168.1.0
10.70.4.13	Class A	255.0.0.0	10.0.0.0

A subnet mask is also able to reference with an indicator known as **Classless Inter-Domain Routing** (**CIDR**), which is defined based on the number of bits. For instance, the subnet mask 255.0.0.0 uses 8 bits (a bit with the value of 0 is considered as unused bits), so it is referenced as /8. Similarly, the subnet mask 255.255.0.0 uses 16 bits and can be referenced as /16, and the subnet mask 255.255.255.0 uses 24 bits and can be referenced as /24. These are the CIDR notations for our previous IP address sample:

IP address	Subnet mask	CIDR notation
174.12.1.8	255.255.0.0	174.12.1.8 /16
192.168.1.15	255.255.255.0	192.168.1.15 /24
10.70.4.13	255.0.0.0	10.70.4.13 /8

Internet Protocol Version 6 – IPv6

IPv6 contains 128 bits and is launched to improve IPv4, which only consists 32 bits. With 32 bits in IPv4, it can address 4,294,967,296 addresses. The number was very high at the beginning, but now it has become insufficient because there are many devices that need an IP address. IPv6 is created to solve the problem because it can address more than 340,000,000,000,000,000,000,000,000,000,000,000,000, or about *3.4028e+38*, which is more than enough—at least for now.

IPv5 had been developed so that it consisted of 64 bits, but it was never adopted because it was believed that the Internet would run out of IP addresses quickly if it was used.

The prominent difference between the IPv4 address and IPv6 address is that instead of displaying the IP address in decimal numbers, IPv6 expresses the address in hexadecimal characters. We can determine whether it is IPv4 or IPv6 at first sight by just looking at this format number. We can call the ipconfig /all command to know our IPv6 address and see it in the Ethernet Adapter Network. I have fe80::f14e:d5e6:aa0a:5855%3, but yours must be different. The address itself is fe80::f14e:d5e6:aa0a:5855, and the last %3 variable is a zone index that is used to identify the network interface card. The number fe80 in the first IPv6 address is stated as a link-local address, which is an IP address that is automatically assigned on the network because it is not automatically configured by DHCP or has not been manually configured yet.

As we know, IPv6 is actually a set of 128 bits and converts its bits into a hexadecimal character in order to simplify its notation. Consider that we have a set of binary digits that form IPv6, as follows:

```
0010 0000 0000 0001 0000 0000 0000 0000
0000 0000 0000 0000 0000 0000 0000 0000
0000 0000 0100 1111 0000 1001 0111 0011
1111 0101 1111 1110 1111 1000 1011 0110
```

Instead of memorizing all these digits, it is easier if we convert it into the IPv6 address format. First, we convert each four digits group into a hexadecimal character and we will get these hexadecimal characters:

```
2001000000000000004f0973f5fef8b6
```

Second, we separate each set of four characters with a colon, as follows:

```
2001:0000:0000:0000:004f:0973:f5fe:f8b6
```

Third, we can throw out the leading zero in each four digit collection, as follows:

```
2001:0:0:0:4f:973:f5fe:f8b6
```

Fourth, we collapse the consecutive zero groups into an empty group, shown as follows:

```
2001::4f:973:f5fe:f8b6
```

Now it is easier for us to memorize this IPv6 address.

> An empty group, which is indicated by two colons (::), means inserting as many as zeros as needed to form this address into 128 bits. IPv6 address is not allowed to have more than one empty group since it will be confusing for us to determine how many zeros there are in each empty group.

Similarly, with IPv4, which classifies the IP address by looking at the first number (the first two bit actually), the type of IPv6 can also be identified by looking at its **prefix**. This is how we write all the addresses that have a network ID `2001:04fe` that begins with a 32-bit prefix:

```
2001:04fe:: /32
```

This means that the first 32 bits of all addresses are 0010 0000 0000 0001 000 0100 1111 1110. However, to ease the reading of this address, we use a hexadecimal character instead.

Using TCP/IP tools for troubleshooting

Some of the following commands can be used to track any TCP/IP errors. The commands can be used to examine whether or not any router is down or any connection is established. It will then help us a lot to decide on the proper solution.

The ipconfig command

We used the `ipconfig` command earlier to identify the MAC address and the IP address. In addition to this, we can use this command to check the TCP/IP configuration. We can also use this command as explained in the upcoming sections.

Displaying the full configuration information

To display the configuration information completely, we can call the following command on the console:

```
ipconfig /all
```

All the configuration information about the network adapter will be displayed for us, such as the network interface card, wireless card, and Ethernet adapter, like we have already tried in *The Data Link layer* section in this chapter when we looked for MAC Address.

Displaying DNS

The following command will display the content of the DNS Resolver Cache using the following option:

```
ipconfig /displaydns
```

By calling the preceding command, we will be provided with the information about DNS in our local system, as follows:

```
Windows IP Configuration

    ipv4only.arpa
    ----------------------------------------
    Record Name . . . . . : ipv4only.arpa
    Record Type . . . . . : 1
    Time To Live  . . . . : 77871
    Data Length . . . . . : 4
    Section . . . . . . . : Answer
```

```
A (Host) Record . . . . : 192.0.0.170

Record Name . . . . . : ipv4only.arpa
Record Type . . . . . : 1
Time To Live  . . . . : 77871
Data Length . . . . . : 4
Section . . . . . . . : Answer
A (Host) Record . . . : 192.0.0.171

ieonlinews.microsoft.com
-----------------------------------------
Record Name . . . . . : ieonlinews.microsoft.com
Record Type . . . . . : 1
Time To Live  . . . . : 307
Data Length . . . . . : 4
Section . . . . . . . : Answer
A (Host) Record . . . : 131.253.34.240
```

The meaning of each field in the output of displaying DNS is as follows:

- **Record Name**: This is the name of the DNS that is to be associated with the IP address.
- **Record Type**: This is the type of the record and is represented as a number.
- **Time To Live**: This is the cache expired time in seconds.
- **Data Length**: This is the size of the memory to store the text of a record value in byte.
- **Section**: If the value is Answer, this means that it replies the actual query, but if the value is Additional, this means that it contains information that will be needed to find the actual answer.
- **A (Host) Record**: This is the place where the actual value is stored.

Flushing DNS

The following command is used to remove the resolved DNS server item but not the item in a cache. Type the following command in the command prompt:

```
ipconfig /flushdns
```

Once it successfully flushes the DNS Resolver Cache, we will be showed this message in the console:

```
Successfully flushed the DNS Resolver Cache.
```

If we call the `ipconfig /displaydns` command again, the resolved DNS server has been removed and remaining are the item in the cache.

Renewing the IP address

There are two commands that can be used to renew an IP address, which are:

```
ipconfig /renew
```

The preceding command will renew the lease process of IPv4 from a DHCP server, while the following command will renew the lease process of IPv6:

```
ipconfig /renew6
```

Releasing the IP address

Use the following two commands to release the lease process of IPv4 and IPv6 respectively, which is obtained from the DHCP server:

```
ipconfig /release
ipconfig /release6
```

These commands only affect the DHCP-assigned (automatically assigned) IP address.

The ping command

The `ping` command is used to examine the connectivity with other computers. It uses **Internet Control Message Protocol (ICMP)** to send a message to target computers. We can use the IP address and hostname to ping the target. Suppose we have a device whose hostname is HOST1, to ping itself, we can use the following command:

```
ping HOST1
```

Then, we will get the following output in our console window:

```
Pinging HOST1 [fe80::f14e:d5e6:aa0a:5855%3] with 32 bytes of data:
Reply from fe80::f14e:d5e6:aa0a:5855%3: time<1ms
Reply from fe80::f14e:d5e6:aa0a:5855%3: time<1ms
Reply from fe80::f14e:d5e6:aa0a:5855%3: time<1ms
Reply from fe80::f14e:d5e6:aa0a:5855%3: time<1ms


Ping statistics for fe80::f14e:d5e6:aa0a:5855%3:
    Packets: Sent = 4, Received = 4, Lost = 0 (0% loss),
Approximate round trip times in milli-seconds:
    Minimum = 0ms, Maximum = 0ms, Average = 0ms
```

If we get the IPv6 address and we want to display it in the IPv4 address instead, we can use the -4 option to force the use of an IPv4 address, as shown in the following code:

```
ping HOST1 -4
```

Then, we will get the output, as follows:

```
Pinging HOST1 [10.1.6.165] with 32 bytes of data:
Reply from 10.1.6.165: bytes=32 time<1ms TTL=128
Reply from 10.1.6.165: bytes=32 time<1ms TTL=128
Reply from 10.1.6.165: bytes=32 time<1ms TTL=128
Reply from 10.1.6.165: bytes=32 time<1ms TTL=128


Ping statistics for 10.1.6.165:
    Packets: Sent = 4, Received = 4, Lost = 0 (0% loss),
Approximate round trip times in milli-seconds:
    Minimum = 0ms, Maximum = 0ms, Average = 0ms
```

However, what if we are displayed the IPv4 address and we need to get inside the IPv6 address instead? We can use the -6 option to force the use of an IPv6 address, as follows:

```
ping HOST1 -6
```

From the `ping` command, there are two points that occur. First, the computer named HOST1 is resolved to the IP address 10.1.6.165. If the hostname resolution does not work, we will get an error like this:

```
Ping request could not find host HOST1. Please check the name and try
again.
```

Second, this command sends four packets to HOST1 and receives four packets. This reply expresses that the computer named HOST1 is working properly and is able to respond to the command request. If HOST1 does not work or is disabled to respond to the request, we will see an output as follows:

```
Pinging HOST1 [10.1.6.165] with 32 bytes of data:

Request timed out.

Request timed out.

Request timed out.

Request timed out.

Ping statistics for 192.168.1.112:
    Packets: Sent = 4, Received = 0, Lost = 4 (100% loss),
```

There is some error information that we may encounter when we send the `ping` command, some of which are as follows:

- **Destination Host Unreachable**: This indicates that there is a problem with the routing. This might be because of the misconfiguration of the default gateway in the local computer or remote computer.

- **TTL Expired in Transit**: This indicates that the ping process has passed through the number of routers that is greater than the TTL (Time To Live) value. Every time the ping passes through a router, the TTL value will be decremented. If the total number of router that a ping has to pass through is more than the TTL value, this error message will be displayed.

Another option that we can use in the ping command is -t. With this option, instead of sending four packets, the `ping` command will continue to send packets until the user stops the same by pressing *Ctrl + C*. This is usually used when we wait for the disconnect status to turn to the connected status. We can send the command to the console, as follows:

```
ping HOST1 -t
```

The tracert command

When we have more than one router, we can use the `tracert` command to trace the path that is taken by the packets. The `tracert` command is similar to the `ping` command, except that `tracert` has the information about the router between the source device and the destination device. Here is the command that I used to trace the communication track from my device to `google.com`:

```
tracert google.com
```

I got this output in my console window:

```
Tracing route to google.com [173.194.126.32]
over a maximum of 30 hops:

 1     1 ms      1 ms      1 ms   254.1.168.192.in-addr.arpa
       [192.168.1.254]
 2    23 ms     26 ms        *    125.166.200.1
 3      *         *       331 ms   189.subnet125-160-
11.speedy.telkom.net.id [125.1
60.11.189]
 4   293 ms     76 ms      84 ms   73.171.94.61.in-addr.arpa
       [61.94.171.73]
 5   504 ms    612 ms     612 ms   61.94.117.229
 6   698 ms    714 ms     209 ms   42.193.240.180.in-addr.arpa
       [180.240.193.42]
 7      *         *          *     Request timed out.
 8      *         *          *     Request timed out.
 9      *       668 ms     512 ms   190.221.14.72.in-addr.arpa
       [72.14.221.190]
10      *         *          *     Request timed out.
11      *         *       582 ms   136.142.85.209.in-addr.arpa
       [209.85.142.136]
12   184 ms    202 ms     202 ms   233.242.85.209.in-addr.arpa
       [209.85.242.233]
13      *         *       563 ms   241.251.85.209.in-addr.arpa
       [209.85.251.241]
14   273 ms     96 ms      83 ms   kul01s08-in-f0.1e100.net
       [173.194.126.32]


Trace complete.
```

As you can see, there are 14 rows, and each row represents a **hop** (a circumstance in which the ping command passes the router). If we divide one row by a column, for instance the fourth row, we will get the following table:

Hop #	RTT1	RTT2	RTT3	Name/IP address
4	293 ms	76 ms	84 ms	73.171.94.61.in-addr.arpa [61.94.171.73]

The explanation of each row is as follows:

- **The Hop number**: This is the first column and is just the number of hops along the route.

- **RTT columns**: This is the **Round Trip Time (RTT)** for our packet to reach that destination and return to our computer. The RRT is bifurcated into three columns because the tracecert command sends three separate signal packets. This is to display the consistency, or a lack of it thereof, in the route.

- **The domain/IP column**: This is the IP address of the router. The domain name will also be informed if it is available.

The pathping command

The pathping command is used to verify the routed path. It examines the route of two devices just like the tracert command does, and then checks the connectivity in each router like the ping command does. The pathping command sends 100 request commands to each router and expects to get 100 replies back. For every request that is not replied, the pathping command will count it as 1 percent data loss. So if, for instance, there are ten requests that do not reply back, there will be 10 percent data loss. The smaller the percentage of data loss, the better connection we have.

We will try to send the pathping command to google.com with the help of the following command:

```
pathping google.com
```

By doing this, we will get the output as follows:

```
Tracing route to google.com [173.194.126.67]
over a maximum of 30 hops:
  0  HOST1 [10.1.7.101]
  1  10.1.7.1
  2  ns.csl-group.net [192.168.2.4]
  3  101.255.54.25
  4  115.124.80.209
```

```
 5   peer-Exch-D2-out.tachyon.net.id [115.124.80.73]

 6   ip-sdi.net.id [103.11.31.1]

 7   ip-31-253.sdi.net.id [103.11.31.253]

 8   209.85.243.158

 9   216.239.40.129

10   209.85.242.243

11   209.85.251.175

12   kul06s05-in-f3.1e100.net [173.194.126.67]
```

```
Computing statistics for 300 seconds...
            Source to Here   This Node/Link
Hop  RTT    Lost/Sent = Pct  Lost/Sent = Pct  Address
 0                                             HOST1 [10.1.7.101]
                             0/ 100 =  0%  |
 1   33ms   1/ 100 =  1%     1/ 100 =  1%  10.1.7.1
                             0/ 100 =  0%  |
 2   24ms   1/ 100 =  1%     1/ 100 =  1%  ns.csl-group.net
     [192.168.2.4]
                             0/ 100 =  0%  |
 3   19ms   1/ 100 =  1%     1/ 100 =  1%  101.255.54.25
                             0/ 100 =  0%  |
 4   18ms   1/ 100 =  1%     1/ 100 =  1%  115.124.80.209
                             0/ 100 =  0%  |
 5   33ms   1/ 100 =  1%     1/ 100 =  1%  peer-Exch-D2-
     out.tachyon.net.id [115.124.80.73]
                             0/ 100 =  0%  |
 6   53ms   0/ 100 =  0%     0/ 100 =  0%  ip-sdi.net.id
     [103.11.31.1]
                             0/ 100 =  0%  |
 7   38ms   2/ 100 =  2%     2/ 100 =  2%  ip-31-253.sdi.net.id
     [103.11.31.253]
                             0/ 100 =  0%  |
 8   44ms   1/ 100 =  1%     1/ 100 =  1%  209.85.243.158
                             0/ 100 =  0%  |
 9   59ms   0/ 100 =  0%     0/ 100 =  0%  216.239.40.129
                             4/ 100 =  4%  |
10   ---    100/ 100 =100%   96/ 100 = 96%  209.85.242.243
                             0/ 100 =  0%  |
11   ---    100/ 100 =100%   96/ 100 = 96%  209.85.251.175
```

```
                                  0/ 100 =  0%    |
12    62ms      4/ 100 =  4%      0/ 100 =  0%  kul06s05-in-
   f3.1e100.net [173.194.126.67]
```

Trace complete.

In the 10th and 11th rows, we get 100 percent packet loss because 100 of the packets sent to the network were lost. However, this is not likely because the data does not arrive at the destination router as ICMP is blocked by the routers. With this command, we can identify in which specific router we will encounter the large percentage of data loss, especially in a large network with many routers connected.

We can also change the number of requests to be sent to the router using the -q option. We just need to state the new number of requests after the option, as follows:

```
pathping -q 10 google.com
```

This will send ten requests to the router instead of 100 requests and will be faster.

The netstat command

The netstat (stands for **network statistics**) command is used to view the TCP/IP statistics by displaying all the information about the TCP/IP connection in the current device. It will show information about connections, ports, and applications that are involved in the network. We can use this command by typing it in the console window:

```
netstat
```

After this, we will get something as shown in the following output:

```
Active Connections
```

Proto	Local Address	Foreign Address	State
TCP	127.0.0.1:50239	HOST1:50240	ESTABLISHED
TCP	127.0.0.1:50240	HOST1:50239	ESTABLISHED
TCP	127.0.0.1:50242	HOST1:50243	ESTABLISHED
TCP	127.0.0.1:50243	HOST1:50242	ESTABLISHED
TCP	127.0.0.1:60855	HOST1:60856	ESTABLISHED
TCP	127.0.0.1:60856	HOST1:60855	ESTABLISHED
TCP	127.0.0.1:60845	HOST1:60846	ESTABLISHED
TCP	127.0.0.1:60846	HOST1:60845	ESTABLISHED
TCP	192.168.1.4:50257	a72-246-188-35:http	ESTABLISHED

TCP	192.168.1.4:50258	a72-246-188-35:http	ESTABLISHED
TCP	192.168.1.4:50259	a72-246-188-35:http	ESTABLISHED
TCP	192.168.1.4:50260	a104-78-107-69:http	ESTABLISHED
TCP	192.168.1.4:50261	a72-246-188-35:http	TIME_WAIT
TCP	192.168.1.4:50262	a72-246-188-35:http	ESTABLISHED
TCP	192.168.1.4:50263	151:http	SYN_SENT
TCP	[::1]:12372	HOST1:49567	ESTABLISHED
TCP	[::1]:49567	HOST1:12372	ESTABLISHED

We can see that there are four columns in the netstat command's output. The explanation of each column is as follows:

- **Proto**: This displays the name of the protocol, which is TCP or UDP.
- **Local Address**: This displays the IP address of the local computer along with the port number being used. If the server is listening on all interfaces, the asterisk symbol (*) will be shown as the hostname. If the port has not been established yet, the port number will be shown as an asterisk as well.
- **Foreign Address**: This displays the IP address and port number of the remote computer to which the socket is connected. If the port has not been established yet, the port number will be shown as an asterisk (*).
- **State**: This indicates the state of a TCP connection. The possible states that we will get are as follows:
  - **SYN_SEND**: This indicates active open systems.
  - **SYN_RECEIVED**: This indicates that the server just received SYN from the client.
  - **ESTABLISHED**: This indicates that the client received the server's SYN and that the session is established.
  - **LISTEN**: This indicates that the server is ready to accept the connection.
  - **FIN_WAIT_1**: This indicates active close systems.
  - **TIMED_WAIT**: This indicates that the client enters this state after active close.
  - **CLOSE_WAIT**: This indicates passive close, which means that the server just received its first FIN from a client.
  - **FIN_WAIT_2**: This indicates that the client just received an acknowledgment of its first FIN from the server.
  - **LAST_ACK**: This indicates that the server is in this state when it sends its own FIN.

○ **CLOSED**: This indicates that the server received ACK from the client and that the connection is now closed.

For more details and information about these states, you can go to `tools.ietf.org/html/rfc793` and refer to *Chapter 3, Functional Specification*.

The telnet command

The `telnet` (stands for **Terminal Network**) command is used to access remote computers over the TCP/IP network. In Windows, there are two Telnet features, which are the Telnet Server and Telnet Client. The former is used to configure Windows in order to listen for incoming connections and allow others to use it. Whereas, the latter is used to connect through Telnet with any server.

By default, Telnet is not installed on the Windows system because of the security risks. It is more secure to keep Telnet disabled since an attacker can check the opening port on the system using Telnet. However, no one can stop us from installing it in our system. We can by do so by performing these steps:

1. Open the **Run** window by pressing *Windows + R*, type `%SYSTEMROOT%\System32\OptionalFeatures.exe` in the text box, and then press the **OK** button. The **Windows Features** window will open then.

2. Check **Telnet Client** and **Telnet Server** options, and then press the **OK** button to confirm the change. The checked option will look like the following screenshot:

Telnet should be installed by now on our computer. Open the Command Prompt window and run the following command to start Telnet:

```
telnet
```

After pressing *Enter*, you will be showed the following output with the blinking cursor at the end:

```
Welcome to Microsoft Telnet Client
Escape Character is 'CTRL+]'
Microsoft Telnet>_
```

Now, Telnet is ready to receive our command. To test it, we can run various commands in it. The complete list of the commands that are available in telnet can be found at windows.microsoft.com/en-us/windows/telnet-commands.

Summary

In this chapter, we came to know the main role of each layer in both the OSI and TCP/IP models when we talked about network architecture. We explored the Internet Protocol and were able to distinguish the difference between IPv4 and IPv6. We were also able to determine the subnet mask and classify the IP address. Moreover, we were able to detect whether an error occurs using various TCP/IP tools.

In the next chapter, we are going to talk about the Boost C++ library, which is the library that will make us more productive in the C++ programming. Now, let's prepare our programming tool and go to the next chapter.

3
Introducing the Boost C++ Libraries

Many programmers use libraries since this simplifies the programming process. Because they do not need to write the function from scratch anymore, using a library can save much code development time. In this chapter, we are going to get acquainted with Boost C++ libraries. Let us prepare our own compiler and text editor to prove the power of Boost libraries. As we do so, we will discuss the following topics:

- Introducing the C++ standard template library
- Introducing the Boost libraries
- Preparing the Boost C++ libraries in MinGW compiler
- Building the Boost libraries
- Compiling code that contains Boost C++ libraries

Introducing the C++ standard template library

The C++ **Standard Template Library** (**STL**) is a generic template-based library that offers generic containers, among other things. Instead of dealing with dynamic arrays, linked lists, binary trees, or hash tables, programmers can easily use an algorithm that is provided by STL.

The STL is structured by containers, iterators, and algorithms, and their roles are as follows:

- **Containers**: Their main role is to manage the collection of objects of certain kinds, such as arrays of integers or linked lists of strings.

- **Iterators**: Their main role is to step through the element of the collections. The working of an iterator is similar to that of a pointer. We can increment the iterator by using the ++ operator and access the value by using the * operator.

- **Algorithms**: Their main role is to process the element of collections. An algorithm uses an iterator to step through all elements. After it iterates the elements, it processes each element, for example, modifying the element. It can also search and sort the element after it finishes iterating all the elements.

Let us examine the three elements that structure STL by creating the following code:

```cpp
/* stl.cpp */
#include <vector>
#include <iostream>
#include <algorithm>

int main(void) {
  int temp;
  std::vector<int> collection;
  std::cout << "Please input the collection of integer numbers,
  input 0 to STOP!\n";
  while(std::cin >> temp != 0) {
    if(temp == 0) break;
    collection.push_back(temp);
  }
  std::sort(collection.begin(), collection.end());
  std::cout << "\nThe sort collection of your integer numbers:\n";
  for(int i: collection) {
    std::cout << i << std::endl;
  }
}
```

Name the preceding code `stl.cpp`, and run the following command to compile it:

```
g++ -Wall -ansi -std=c++11 stl.cpp -o stl
```

Before we dissect this code, let us run it to see what happens. This program will ask users to enter as many as integer they want, and then it will sort the numbers. To stop the input and ask the program to start sorting, the user has to input 0. This means that 0 will not be included in the sorting process. Since we do not prevent users from entering non-integer numbers such as 3.14, the program will soon stop waiting for the next number after the user enters a non-integer number. The code yields the following output:

We have entered six integers: 43, 7, 568, 91, 2240, and 56. The last entry is 0 in order to stop the input process. Then the program starts to sort the numbers and we get the numbers sorted in sequential order: 7, 43, 56, 91, 568, and 2240.

Now, let us examine our code to identify the containers, iterators, and algorithms that are contained in the STL:

```
std::vector<int> collection;
```

The preceding code snippet has containers from STL. There are several containers, and we use a **vector** in the code. A vector manages its elements in a dynamic array, and they can be accessed randomly and directly with the corresponding index. In our code, the container is prepared to hold integer numbers so we have to define the type of the value inside the angle brackets `<int>`. These angle brackets are also called **generics** in STL:

```
collection.push_back(temp);
std::sort(collection.begin(), collection.end());
```

The `begin()` and `end()` functions in the preceding code are algorithms in STL. They play the role of processing the data in the containers that are used to get the first and the last elements in the container. Before that, we can see the `push_back()` function, which is used to append an element to the container:

```
for(int i: collection) {
  std::cout << i << std::endl;
}
```

The preceding `for` block will iterate each element of the integer that is called as `collection`. Each time the element is iterated, we can process the element separately. In the preceding example, we showed the number to the user. That is how the iterators in STL play their role.

```
#include <vector>
#include <algorithm>
```

We include vector definition to define all `vector` functions and `algorithm` definition to invoke the `sort()` function.

Introducing the Boost C++ libraries

The Boost C++ libraries is a set of libraries to complement the C++ standard libraries. The set contains more than a hundred libraries that we can use to increase our productivity in C++ programming. It is also used when our requirements go beyond what is available in the STL. It provides source code under Boost Licence, which means that it allows us to use, modify, and distribute the libraries for free, even for commercial use.

The development of Boost is handled by the Boost community, which consists of C++ developers from around the world. The mission of the community is to develop high-quality libraries as a complement to STL. Only proven libraries will be added to the Boost libraries.

For detailed information about Boost libraries, go to www.boost.org. And if you want to contribute developing libraries to Boost, you can join the developer mailing list at lists.boost.org/mailman/listinfo. cgi/boost.

The entire source code of the libraries is available on the official GitHub page at github.com/boostorg.

Advantages of Boost libraries

As we know, using Boost libraries will increase programmer productivity. Moreover, by using Boost libraries, we will get advantages such as these:

- It is open source, so we can inspect the source code and modify it if needed.

- Its license allows us to develop both open source and close source projects. It also allows us to commercialize our software freely.

- It is well documented and we can find it libraries all explained, along with sample code from the official site.

- It supports almost any modern operating system, such as Windows and Linux. It also supports many popular compilers.

- It is a complement to STL instead of a replacement. It means using Boost libraries will ease those programming processes that are not handled by STL yet. In fact, many parts of Boost are included in the standard C++ library.

Preparing Boost libraries for the MinGW compiler

Before we go through to program our C++ application by using Boost libraries, the libraries need to be configured in order to be recognized by MinGW compiler. Here, we are going to prepare our programming environment so that our compiler is able use Boost libraries.

Downloading Boost libraries

The best source from which to download Boost is the official download page. We can go there by pointing our internet browser to www.boost.org/users/download. Find the **Download** link in **Current Release** section. At the time of writing, the current version of Boost libraries is 1.58.0, but when you read this book, the version may have changed. If so, you can still choose the current release because the higher version must be compatible with the lower. However, you have to adjust as we're going to talk about the setting later. Otherwise, choosing the same version will make it easy for you to follow all the instructions in this book.

There are four file formats to be choose from for download; they are `.zip`, `.tar.gz`, `.tar.bz2`, and `.7z`. There is no difference among the four files but their file size. The largest file size is of the ZIP format and the lowest is that of the 7Z format. Because of the file size, Boost recommends that we download the 7Z format. See the following image for comparison:

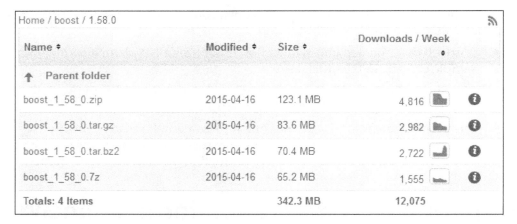

Home / boost / 1.58.0					
Name ⬍	Modified ⬍	Size ⬍	Downloads / Week ⬍		
⬆ Parent folder					
boost_1_58_0.zip	2015-04-16	123.1 MB	4,816		ⓘ
boost_1_58_0.tar.gz	2015-04-16	83.6 MB	2,982		ⓘ
boost_1_58_0.tar.bz2	2015-04-16	70.4 MB	2,722		ⓘ
boost_1_58_0.7z	2015-04-16	65.2 MB	1,555		ⓘ
Totals: 4 Items		342.3 MB	12,075		

From the preceding image, we can see the size of ZIP version is 123.1 MB while the size of the 7Z version is 65.2 MB. It means that the size of the ZIP version is almost twice that of the 7Z version. Therefore, they suggest that you choose the 7Z format to reduce download and decompression time. Let us choose `boost_1_58_0.7z` to be downloaded and save it to our local storage.

Deploying Boost libraries

After we have got `boost_1_58_0.7z` in our local storage, decompress it using the 7ZIP application and save the decompression files to `C:\boost_1_58_0`.

[The 7ZIP application can be grabbed from www.7-zip.org/download.html.]

The directory then should contain file structures as follows:

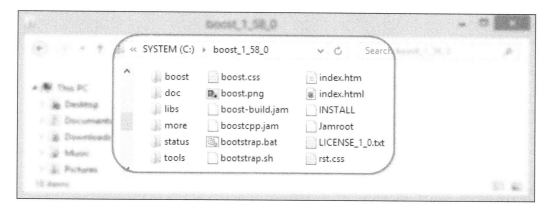

 Instead of browsing to the Boost download page and searching for the Boost version manually, we can go directly to `sourceforge.net/projects/boost/files/boost/1.58.0`. It will be useful when the 1.58.0 version is no longer the current release.

Using Boost libraries

Most libraries in Boost are **header-only**; this means that all declarations and definitions of functions, including namespaces and macros, are visible to the compiler and there is no need to compile them separately. We can now try to use Boost with the program to convert the string into `int` value as follows:

```cpp
/* lexical.cpp */
#include <boost/lexical_cast.hpp>
#include <string>
#include <iostream>

int main(void) {
  try     {
    std::string str;
    std::cout << "Please input first number: ";
    std::cin >> str;
    int n1 = boost::lexical_cast<int>(str);
    std::cout << "Please input second number: ";
    std::cin >> str;
```

```
    int n2 = boost::lexical_cast<int>(str);
    std::cout << "The sum of the two numbers is ";
    std::cout << n1 + n2 << "\n";
    return 0;
  }
  catch (const boost::bad_lexical_cast &e) {
    std::cerr << e.what() << "\n";
    return 1;
  }
}
```

Open the Notepad++ application, type the preceding code, and save it as `lexical.cpp` in `C:\CPP`— the directory we had created in *Chapter 1, Simplifying Your Network Programming in C++*. Now open the command prompt, point the active directory to `C:\CPP`, and then type the following command:

g++ -Wall -ansi lexical.cpp -Ic:\boost_1_58_0 -o lexical

We have a new option here, which is `-I` (the "include" option). This option is used along with the full path of the directory to inform the compiler that we have another header directory that we want to include to our code. Since we store our Boost libraries in `c:\ boost_1_58_0`, we can use `-Ic:\boost_1_58_0` as an additional parameter.

In `lexical.cpp`, we apply `boost::lexical_cast` to convert `string` type data into `int` type data. The program will ask the user to input two numbers and will then automatically find the sum of both numbers. If a user inputs an inappropriate number, it will inform them that an error has occurred.

The `Boost.LexicalCast` library is provided by Boost for casting one data type to another (converting numeric types such as `int`, `double`, or `floats` into `string` types, and vice versa). Now, let us dissect `lexical.cpp` to for a more detailed understanding of what it does:

```
#include <boost/lexical_cast.hpp>
#include <string>
#include <iostream>
```

We include `boost/lexical_cast.hpp` in order to be able to invoke `boost::lexical_cast` function since the function is declared in `lexical_cast.hpp`. Also we use `string` header to apply `std::string` function as well as `iostream` header to apply `std::cin`, `std::cout` and `std::cerr` function.

Other functions, such as `std::cin` and `std::cout`, have been talked about in *Chapter 1, Simplifying Your Network Programming in C++*, and we saw what their functions are so we can skip those lines:

```
int n1 = boost::lexical_cast<int>(str);
int n2 = boost::lexical_cast<int>(str);
```

We used the preceding two separate lines to convert the user-provided input `string` into the `int` data type. Then, after converting the data type, we summed up both of the `int` values.

We can also see the `try-catch` block in the preceding code. It is used to catch the error if user inputs an inappropriate number, except 0 to 9.

```
catch (const boost::bad_lexical_cast &e)
{
  std::cerr << e.what() << "\n";
  return 1;
}
```

The preceding code snippet will catch errors and inform the user what exactly the error message is by using `boost::bad_lexical_cast`. We call the `e.what()` function to obtain the string of the error message.

Now let us run the application by typing `lexical` at the command prompt. We will get output like the following:

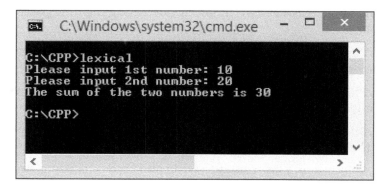

I put 10 for first input and 20 for the second input. The result is 30 because it just sums up both input. But what will happen if I put in a non-numerical value, for instance Packt. Here is the output to try that condition:

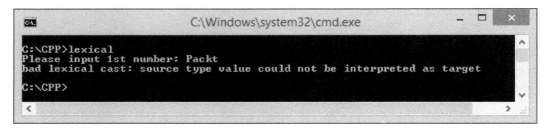

Once the application found the error, it will ignore the next statement and go directly to the catch block. By using the e.what() function, the application can get the error message and show it to the user. In our example, we obtain bad lexical cast: source type value could not be interpreted as target as the error message because we try to assign the string data to int type variable.

Building Boost libraries

As we discussed previously, most libraries in Boost are header-only, but not all of them. There are some libraries that have to be built separately. They are:

- Boost.Chrono: This is used to show the variety of clocks, such as current time, the range between two times, or calculating the time passed in the process.

- Boost.Context: This is used to create higher-level abstractions, such as coroutines and cooperative threads.

- Boost.Filesystem: This is used to deal with files and directories, such as obtaining the file path or checking whether a file or directory exists.

- Boost.GraphParallel: This is an extension to the **Boost Graph Library** (**BGL**) for parallel and distributed computing.

- Boost.IOStreams: This is used to write and read data using stream. For instance, it loads the content of a file to memory or writes compressed data in GZIP format.

- Boost.Locale: This is used to localize the application, in other words, translate the application interface to user's language.

- Boost.MPI: This is used to develop a program that executes tasks concurrently. **MPI itself stands for Message Passing Interface**.

- `Boost.ProgramOptions`: This is used to parse command-line options. Instead of using the `argv` variable in the `main` parameter, it uses double minus (`--`) to separate each command-line option.

- `Boost.Python`: This is used to parse Python language in C++ code.

- `Boost.Regex`: This is used to apply regular expression in our code. But if our development supports C++11, we do not depend on the `Boost.Regex` library anymore since it is available in the `regex` header file.

- `Boost.Serialization`: This is used to convert objects into a series of bytes that can be saved and then restored again into the same object.

- `Boost.Signals`: This is used to create signals. The signal will trigger an event to run a function on it.

- `Boost.System`: This is used to define errors. It contains four classes: `system::error_code`, `system::error_category`, `system::error_condition`, and `system::system_error`. All of these classes are inside the `boost` namespace. It is also supported in the C++11 environment, but because many Boost libraries use `Boost.System`, it is necessary to keep including `Boost.System`.

- `Boost.Thread`: This is used to apply threading programming. It provides classes to synchronize access on multiple-thread data. In C++11 environments, the `Boost.Thread` library offers extensions, so we can interrupt thread in `Boost.Thread`.

- `Boost.Timer`: This is used to measure the code performance by using clocks. It measures time passed based on usual clock and CPU time, which states how much time has been spent to execute the code.

- `Boost.Wave`: This provides a reusable C preprocessor that we can use in our C++ code.

There are also a few libraries that have optional, separately compiled binaries. They are as follows:

- `Boost.DateTime`: It is used to process time data; for instance, calendar dates and time. It has a binary component that is only needed if we use `to_string`, `from_string`, or serialization features. It is also needed if we target our application in Visual C++ 6.x or Borland.

- `Boost.Graph`: It is used to create two-dimensional graphics. It has a binary component that is only needed if we intend to parse `GraphViz` files.

- `Boost.Math`: It is used to deal with mathematical formulas. It has binary components for `cmath` functions.

- Boost.Random: It is used to generate random numbers. It has a binary component, which is only needed if we want to use random_device.

- Boost.Test: It is used to write and organize test programs and their runtime execution. It can be used in header-only or separately compiled mode, but separate compilation is recommended for serious use.

- Boost.Exception: It is used to add data to an exception after it has been thrown. It provides non-intrusive implementation of exception_ptr for 32-bit _MSC_VER==1310 and _MSC_VER==1400, which requires a separately compiled binary. This is enabled by #define BOOST_ENABLE_NON_ INTRUSIVE_EXCEPTION_PTR.

Let us try to recreate the random number generator program we created in *Chapter 1, Simplifying Your Network Programming in C++*. But now we will use the Boost. Random library instead of std::rand() from the C++ standard function. Let us take a look at the following code:

```cpp
/* rangen_boost.cpp */
#include <boost/random/mersenne_twister.hpp>
#include <boost/random/uniform_int_distribution.hpp>
#include <iostream>

int main(void) {
  int guessNumber;
  std::cout << "Select number among 0 to 10: ";
  std::cin >> guessNumber;
  if(guessNumber < 0 || guessNumber > 10) {
    return 1;
  }
  boost::random::mt19937 rng;
  boost::random::uniform_int_distribution<> ten(0,10);
  int randomNumber = ten(rng);
  if(guessNumber == randomNumber) {
    std::cout << "Congratulation, " << guessNumber << " is your
    lucky number.\n";
  }
  else {
    std::cout << "Sorry, I'm thinking about number " <<
    randomNumber << "\n";
  }
  return 0;
}
```

We can compile the preceding source code by using the following command:

```
g++ -Wall -ansi -Ic:/boost_1_58_0 rangen_boost.cpp -o rangen_boost
```

Now, let us run the program. Unfortunately, for the three times that I ran the program, I always obtained the same random number as follows:

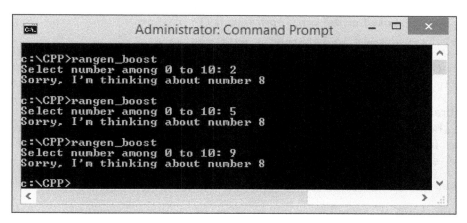

As we can see from this example, we always get number 8. This is because we apply Mersenne Twister, a **Pseudorandom Number Generator (PRNG)**, which uses the default seed as a source of randomness so it will generate the same number every time the program is run. And, of course, it is not the program that we expect.

Now, we will rework the program once again, just in two lines. First, find the following line:

```
#include <boost/random/mersenne_twister.hpp>
```

Change it as follows:

```
#include <boost/random/random_device.hpp>
```

Next, find the following line:

```
boost::random::mt19937 rng;
```

Change it as follows:

```
boost::random::random_device rng;
```

Then, save the file as rangen2_boost.cpp and compile the rangen2_boost.cpp file by using the command like we compiled rangen_boost.cpp. The command will look like this:

```
g++ -Wall -ansi -Ic:/boost_1_58_0 rangen2_boost.cpp -o rangen2_boost
```

Sadly, there will be something wrong and the compiler will show the following error message:

```
cc8KWVvX.o:rangen2_boost.cpp:(.text$_ZN5boost6random6detail20generate
_uniform_intINS0_13random_deviceEjEET0_RT_S4_S4_N4mpl_5bool_ILb1EEE[_
ZN5boost6random6detail20generate_uniform_intINS0_13random_deviceEjEET
0_RT_S4_S4_N4mpl_5bool_ILb1EEE]+0x24f): more undefined references to
boost::random::random_device::operator()()' follow
```

```
collect2.exe: error: ld returned 1 exit status
```

This is because, as we saw earlier, the `Boost.Random` library needs to be compiled separately if we want to use the `random_device` attribute.

Boost libraries have a system to compile or build Boost itself, called `Boost.Build` library. There are two steps we have to achieve to install the `Boost.Build` library. First, run **Bootstrap** by pointing the active directory at the command prompt to `C:\boost_1_58_0` and typing the following command:

`bootstrap.bat mingw`

We use our MinGW compiler we had installed in *Chapter 1, Simplifying Your Network Programming in C++*, as our toolset in compiling the Boost library. Wait a second and then we will get the following output if the process is a success:

```
Building Boost.Build engine

Bootstrapping is done. To build, run:

    .\b2

To adjust configuration, edit 'project-config.jam'.
Further information:

    - Command line help:
    .\b2 --help

    - Getting started guide:
    http://boost.org/more/getting_started/windows.html

    - Boost.Build documentation:
    http://www.boost.org/build/doc/html/index.html
```

In this step, we will find four new files in the Boost library's root directory. They are:

- `b2.exe`: This is an executable file to build Boost libraries
- `bjam.exe`: This is exactly the same as `b2.exe` but it is a legacy version
- `bootstrap.log`: This contains logs from the `bootstrap` process
- `project-config.jam`: This contains a setting that will be used in the building process when we run `b2.exe`

We also find that this step creates a new directory in `C:\boost_1_58_0\tools\build\src\engine\bin.ntx86`, which contains a bunch of `.obj` files associated with Boost libraries that needed to be compiled.

After that, run the second step by typing the following command at the command prompt:

```
b2 install toolset=gcc
```

Grab yourself a cup of coffee after running that command because it will take about twenty to fifty minutes to finish the process, depending on your system specifications. The last output we will get will be as follows:

```
...updated 12562 targets...
```

This means that the process is complete and we have now built the Boost libraries. If we check in our explorer, the `Boost.Build` library adds `C:\boost_1_58_0\stage\lib`, which contains a collection of static and dynamic libraries that we can use directly in our program.

 bootstrap.bat and b2.exe use `msvc` (Microsoft Visual C++ compiler) as the default toolset, and many Windows developers already have `msvc` installed on their machines. Since we have installed the GCC compiler, we set the `mingw` and `gcc` toolset options in Boost's build. If you also have `mvsc` installed and want to use it in Boost's build, the toolset options can be omitted.

Now, let us try to compile the `rangen2_boost.cpp` file again, but now with the following command:

```
c:\CPP>g++ -Wall -ansi -Ic:/boost_1_58_0 rangen2_boost.cpp -
Lc:\boost_1_58_0\stage\lib -lboost_random-mgw49-mt-1_58 -
lboost_system-mgw49-mt-1_58 -o rangen2_boost
```

We have two new options here, they are -L and -l. The -L option is used to define the path that contains the library file if it is not in the active directory. The -l option is used to define the name of library file but omitting the first lib word in front of the file name. In this case, the original library file name is libboost_random-mgw49-mt-1_58.a, and we omit the lib phrase and the file extension for option -l.

The new file called rangen2_boost.exe will be created in C:\CPP. But before we can run the program, we have to ensure that the directory that the program installed has contained two library files which the program is dependent on. These are libboost_random-mgw49-mt-1_58.dll and libboost_system-mgw49-mt-1_58.dll, and we can get them from the library directory c:\boost_1_58_0_1\stage\lib.

Just to make it easy for us to run that program, run the following copy command to copy the two library files to C:\CPP:

```
copy c:\boost_1_58_0_1\stage\lib\libboost_random-mgw49-mt-1_58.dll
c:\cpp
```

```
copy c:\boost_1_58_0_1\stage\lib\libboost_system-mgw49-mt-1_58.dll
c:\cpp
```

And now the program should run smoothly.

In order to create a network application, we are going to use the Boost.Asio library. We do not find Boost.Asio — the library that we are going to use to create a network application — in the non-header-only library. It seems that we do not need to build the Boost library since Boost.Asio is header-only library. This is true, but since Boost.Asio depends on Boost.System and Boost.System needs to be built before being used, it is important to build Boost first before we can use it to create our network application.

 For option -I and -L, the compiler does not care if we use backslash (\) or slash (/) to separate each directory name in the path because the compiler can handle both Windows and Unix path styles.

Summary

We saw that Boost C++ libraries were developed to complement the standard C++ library. We have also been able to set up our MinGW compiler in order to compile the code that contains Boost libraries and build the binaries of libraries that have to be compiled separately. In the next chapter, which talks about the `Boost.Asio` library (the library we are going to use to develop network applications), we will delve into Boost libraries specifically. Please remember that although we can use the `Boost.Asio` library as a header-only library, it would be better to build all Boost libraries by using the `Boost.Build` library. It will be easy for us to use all libraries without worrying about compiling failure.

4
Getting Started with Boost.Asio

We already know about the Boost C++ library in general. Now it is time to find out more about Boost.Asio, the library that we use to develop network applications. Boost.Asio is a collection of libraries that are used to process data asynchronously because Asio itself stands for **Asynchronous I/O (input and output)**. Asynchronous means that a particular task in a program will operate without blocking other tasks and Boost.Asio will notify the program when it has finished carrying out that task. In other words, the task is executed concurrently.

In this chapter, we are going to discuss the following topics:

* Distinguishing between concurrent and nonconcurrent programming
* Understanding the I/O service, the brain and the heart of Boost.Asio
* Binding a function dynamically to a function pointer
* Synchronizing access to any global data or shared data

Getting closer to the Boost.Asio library

Imagine we are developing an audio downloader application and we want the user to be able to navigate to all the menus in the application, even when the downloading process is in progress. If we do not use asynchronous programming, the application will be blocked by the downloading process and the user will have to wait until the downloading of the file is complete. But thanks to asynchronous programming, the user does not need to wait until the download process is complete to continue using the application.

In other words, a synchronous process is like queuing in a theater ticketing line. We will be served only if we reach the ticket counter and before that, we have to wait for all the processes of the previous costumers who are in front of us in the line to be completed. In contrast, we can imagine that the asynchronous process is like dinning in a restaurant where the waiter does not have to wait for the order of a customer to be prepared by the cook. Instead of blocking the time and waiting for the cook, the waiter can go and take orders from other customers.

The Boost libraries also have the Boost.Thread library that is used to execute tasks concurrently, but the Boost.Thread library is used to access internal resources, such as the CPU core resource, while the Boost.Asio library is used to access external resources, such as network connections, because the data is sent and received by a network card.

Let's distinguish between concurrent and nonconcurrent programming. Take a look at the following code for this:

```
/* nonconcurrent.cpp */
#include <iostream>

void Print1(void) {
  for(int i=0; i<5; i++) {
    std::cout << "[Print1] Line: " << i << "\n";
  }
}

void Print2(void) {
  for(int i=0; i<5; i++) {
    std::cout << "[Print2] Line: " << i << "\n";
  }
}

int main(void) {
  Print1();
  Print2();
  return 0;
}
```

The preceding code is a nonconcurrent program. Save the code as nonconcurrent.cpp and then compile it using the following command:

```
g++ -Wall -ansi nonconcurrent.cpp -o nonconcurrent
```

After running `nonconcurrent.cpp`, an output like this will be displayed in front of you:

We want to run two functions: `Print1()` and `Print2()`. In nonconcurrent programming, the application runs the `Print1()` function first and afterwards, completes all the instructions in the function. The program continues to invoke the `Print2()` function until the instruction is run completely.

Now, let's compare nonconcurrent programming with concurrent programming. For this, take a look at the following code:

```cpp
/* concurrent.cpp */
#include <boost/thread.hpp>
#include <boost/chrono.hpp>
#include <iostream>

void Print1() {
  for (int i=0; i<5; i++) {
    boost::this_thread::sleep_for(boost::chrono::
    milliseconds{500});
    std::cout << "[Print1] Line: " << i << '\n';
  }
}

void Print2() {
  for (int i=0; i<5; i++) {
    boost::this_thread::sleep_for(boost::chrono::
    milliseconds{500});
    std::cout << "[Print2] Line: " << i << '\n';
  }
}
```

```
int main(void) {
  boost::thread_group threads;
  threads.create_thread(Print1);
  threads.create_thread(Print2);
  threads.join_all();
}
```

Save the preceding code as `concurrent.cpp` and compile it using the following command:

```
g++ -ansi -std=c++11 -I ../boost_1_58_0 concurrent.cpp -o concurrent
-L ../boost_1_58_0/stage/lib -lboost_system-mgw49-mt-1_58 -lws2_32 -l
boost_thread-mgw49-mt-1_58 -l boost_chrono-mgw49-mt-1_58
```

Run the program to get the following output:

```
C:\Windows\system32\cmd.exe

C:\CPP>g++ -ansi -std=c++11 -I ../boost_1_58_0 concurrent.cpp -o concurrent -L .
./boost_1_58_0/stage/lib -lboost_system-mgw49-mt-1_58 -lws2_32 -l boost_thread-m
gw49-mt-1_58 -l boost_chrono-mgw49-mt-1_58

C:\CPP>concurrent
[Print2] Line: 0
[Print1] Line: 0
[Print2] Line: 1
[Print1] Line: 1
[Print2] Line: 2
[Print1] Line: 2
[Print2] Line: 3
[Print1] Line: 3
[Print1] Line: 4
[Print2] Line: 4

C:\CPP>
```

We can see from the preceding output that the `Print1()` and `Print2()` functions are run concurrently. The `Print2()` function does not need to wait for the `Print1()` function to finish executing all the instructions that are to be invoked. This is why we call this concurrent programming.

> Do not forget to copy the associated dynamic library file if you include a library in your code. For instance, if you include `boost_system-mgw49-mt-1_58` using the `-l` option, you have to copy the `libboost_system-mgw49-mt-1_58.dll` file and paste it into the same directory as the output-executable file.

Examining the I/O service in the Boost. Asio library

The core object of the `Boost::Asio` namespace is `io_service`. The **I/O service** is a channel that is used to access operating system resources and establish communication between our program and the operating system that performs I/O requests. There is also an **I/O object** that has the role of submitting I/O requests. For instance, the `tcp::socket` object will provide a socket programming request from our program to the operating system.

Using and blocking the run() function

One of the most frequently used functions in the I/O service object is the `run()` function. It is used to run the `io_service` object's event processing loop. It will block the next statement program until all the work in the `io_service` object is completed and there are no more handlers to be dispatched. If we stop the `io_service` object, it will no longer block the program.

 In programming, `event` is an action or occurrence detected by a program, which will be handled by the program using the `event handler` object. The `io_service` object has one or more instances where events are handled, which is `event processing loop`.

Now, let's take a look at the following code snippet:

```cpp
/* unblocked.cpp */
#include <boost/asio.hpp>
#include <iostream>

int main(void) {
  boost::asio::io_service io_svc;

  io_svc.run();

  std::cout << "We will see this line in console window." <<
  std::endl;

  return 0;
}
```

We save the preceding code as `unblocked.cpp` and then run the following command to compile it:

```
g++ -Wall -ansi -I ../boost_1_58_0 unblocked.cpp -o unblocked -L
../boost_1_58_0/stage/lib -l boost_system-mgw49-mt-1_58 -l ws2_32
```

When we run the program, the following output gets displayed:

We will see this line in console window.

However, why do we still obtain the line of text in the console even though previously we knew that the `run()` function blocks the next function after it is invoked? This is because we have not given any work to the `io_service` object. Since there is no work for `io_service` to do, the `io_service` object should not block the program.

Now, let's give the `io_service` object some work to do. The program for this will look like as shown in the following code:

```cpp
/* blocked.cpp */
#include <boost/asio.hpp>
#include <iostream>

int main(void) {
  boost::asio::io_service io_svc;
  boost::asio::io_service::work worker(io_svc);

  io_svc.run();

  std::cout << "We will not see this line in console window :(" <<
  std::endl;

  return 0;
}
```

Give the preceding code the name `blocked.cpp` and then compile it by typing the following command in our console window:

```
g++ -Wall -ansi -I ../boost_1_58_0 blocked.cpp -o blocked -L
../boost_1_58_0/stage/lib -l boost_system-mgw49-mt-1_58 -l ws2_32
```

If we run the program by typing `blocked` in our console, we will not see the line of text anymore since we have added the following code line:

```
boost::asio::io_service::work work(io_svc);
```

The work class is responsible for telling the io_service object when the work starts and when it has finished. It will make sure that the run() function in the io_service object will not exit during the time the work is underway. Also, it will make sure that the run() function does exit when there is no unfinished work remaining. In our preceding code, the work class informs the io_service object that it has work to do, but we do not define what the work is. Therefore, the program will be blocked infinitely and it will not show the output. The reason it has been blocked is because the run() function is invoked even though we can still terminate the program by pressing *Ctrl + C*.

Using the non-blocking poll() function

Now, we will leave the run() function for a while and try to use the poll() function. The poll() function is used to run ready handlers until there are no more ready handlers remaining or until the io_service object has been stopped. However, in contrast with the run() function, the poll() function will not block the program.

Let's type the following code that uses the poll() function and save it as poll.cpp:

```
/* poll.cpp */
#include <boost/asio.hpp>
#include <iostream>

int main(void) {
  boost::asio::io_service io_svc;

  for(int i=0; i<5; i++) {
    io_svc.poll();
    std::cout << "Line: " << i << std::endl;
  }

  return 0;
}
```

Then, compile poll.cpp by using the following command:

```
g++ -Wall -ansi -I ../boost_1_58_0 poll.cpp -o poll -L
../boost_1_58_0/stage/lib -l boost_system-mgw49-mt-1_58 -l ws2_32
```

Because there is no work that the `io_service` object has to do, the program should display the five lines of text as follows:

However, what if we give work to the `io_service` object when we use the `poll()` function? To find out the answer, let's type the following code and save it as `pollwork.cpp`:

```
/* pollwork.cpp */
#include <boost/asio.hpp>
#include <iostream>

int main(void) {
  boost::asio::io_service io_svc;
  boost::asio::io_service::work work(io_svc);

  for(int i=0; i<5; i++) {
    io_svc.poll();
    std::cout << "Line: " << i << std::endl;
  }

  return 0;
}
```

To compile `pollwork.cpp`, use the following command:

```
g++ -Wall -ansi -I ../boost_1_58_0 pollwork.cpp -o pollwork -L
../boost_1_58_0/stage/lib -l boost_system-mgw49-mt-1_58 -l ws2_32
```

The difference between the `poll.cpp` file and the `pollwork.cpp` file is only the following line:

```
boost::asio::io_service::work work(io_svc);
```

However, if we run `pollwork.exe`, we will obtain the same output as that of `poll.exe`. This is because, as we know from before, the `poll()` function will not block the program while there is more work to do. It will execute the current work and then return the value.

Removing the work object

We can also unblock the program by removing the `work` object from the `io_service` object, but we have to use a pointer to the `work` object in order to remove the `work` object itself. We are going to use the `shared_ptr` pointer, a smart pointer provided by the `Boost` libraries.

Let's use the modified code of `blocked.cpp`. The code for this will be as follows:

```
/* removework.cpp */
#include <boost/asio.hpp>
#include <boost/shared_ptr.hpp>
#include <iostream>

int main(void) {
  boost::asio::io_service io_svc;
  boost::shared_ptr<boost::asio::io_service::work> worker(
    new boost::asio::io_service::work(io_svc)
  );

  worker.reset();

  io_svc.run();

  std::cout << "We will not see this line in console window :(" <<
  std::endl;

  return 0;
}
```

Save the preceding code as `removework.cpp` and compile it using the following command:

```
g++ -Wall -ansi -I ../boost_1_58_0 removework.cpp -o removework -L
../boost_1_58_0/stage/lib -l boost_system-mgw49-mt-1_58 -l ws2_32
```

When we run `removework.cpp`, compared to `blocked.cpp`, which will block the program infinitely, the following line of text will be displayed to us:

```
                           C:\Windows\system32\cmd.exe                    _ □ ×

C:\CPP>g++ -Wall -ansi -I ../boost_1_58_0 removework.cpp -o removework -L ../boo
st_1_58_0/stage/lib -l boost_system-mgw49-mt-1_58 -l ws2_32

C:\CPP>removework
We will not see this line in console window :<

C:\CPP>
```

Now, let's dissect the code. As we can see in the preceding code, we used the `shared_ptr` pointer to instantiate the `work` object. With this smart pointer provided by Boost, we no longer need to manually delete memory allocation in order to store the pointer since it guarantees that the object pointed to will be deleted when the last pointer is destroyed or reset. Do not forget to include `shared_ptr.hpp` inside the `boost` directory as the `shared_ptr` pointer is defined in the header file.

We also add the `reset()` function to reset the `io_service` object when it prepares for a subsequent `run()` function invocation. The `reset()` function has to be invoked before any invocation of the `run()` or `poll()` functions. It will also tell the `shared_ptr` pointer to automatically destroy the pointer we created. More information about the `share_ptr` pointer can be found at `www.boost.org/doc/libs/1_58_0/libs/smart_ptr/shared_ptr.htm`.

The preceding program explains that we have successfully removed the `work` object from the `io_service` object. We can use this functionality if we intend to finish all the pending work even though it hasn't actually been finished yet.

Dealing with many threads

We have only dealt with one thread for one `io_service` object so far. If we want to deal with more threads in a single `io_service` object, the following code will explain how to do this:

```cpp
/* multithreads.cpp */
#include <boost/asio.hpp>
#include <boost/shared_ptr.hpp>
#include <boost/thread.hpp>
#include <iostream>
```

```
boost::asio::io_service io_svc;
int a = 0;

void WorkerThread() {
  std::cout << ++a << ".\n";
  io_svc.run();
  std::cout << "End.\n";
}

int main(void) {
  boost::shared_ptr<boost::asio::io_service::work> worker(
    new boost::asio::io_service::work(io_svc)
  );

  std::cout << "Press ENTER key to exit!" << std::endl;

  boost::thread_group threads;
  for(int i=0; i<5; i++)
    threads.create_thread(WorkerThread);

  std::cin.get();

  io_svc.stop();

  threads.join_all();

  return 0;
}
```

Give the preceding code the name `mutithreads.cpp` and then compile it using the following command:

```
g++ -Wall -ansi -I ../boost_1_58_0 multithreads.cpp -o multithreads -
L ../boost_1_58_0/stage/lib -l boost_system-mgw49-mt-1_58 -l ws2_32 -
l boost_thread-mgw49-mt-1_58
```

We include the `thread.hpp` header file so that we can use the `thread` object defined inside the header file. The thread itself is a piece sequence of instructions that can be run independently, so we can run multiple threads at once.

Now, run `mutithreads.exe` in our console. I obtained the following output by running it:

You might obtain a different output because all the threads that are set up as a pool of threads are equivalent to each other. The `io_service` object may choose any one of them randomly and invoke its handler, so we cannot guarantee whether or not the `io_service` object will choose a thread sequentially:

```
for(int i=0; i<5; i++)
    threads.create_thread(WorkerThread);
```

Using the preceding code snippet, we can create five threads to display lines of text as you can see in the previous screenshot. The five lines of text will be enough for this example to view the order of nonconcurrent flow:

```
std::cout << ++a << ".\n";
io_svc.run();
```

In every thread that is created, the program will invoke the `run()` function to run the work of the `io_service` object. Calling the `run()` function once is insufficient because all nonworkers will be invoked after the `run()` object finishes all its work.

After creating five threads, the program runs the work of the `io_service` object:

```
std::cin.get();
```

After all the work is run, the program waits for you to press the *Enter* key from the keyboard using the preceding code snippet:

```
io_svc.stop();
```

Once the user presses the *Enter* key, the program will hit the preceding code snippet. The `stop()` function will notify the `io_service` object that all the work should be stopped. This means that the program will stop the five threads that we have:

```
threads.join_all();
```

The `join_all()` function will then continue with all the unfinished threads, and the program will wait until all the processes in all the threads are complete. The preceding code snippet will continue the following statement inside the `WorkerThread()` block:

```
std::cout << "End.\n";
```

So after we press the *Enter* key, the program will finish its remaining code and we will obtain the rest of the output as follows:

Understanding the Boost.Bind library

We have been able to use the `io_service` object and initialize the `work` object. What we should know after this is how to give some work to the `io_service` object. But before we progress to giving work to the `io_service` service, we need to understand the `boost::bind` library.

The `Boost.Bind` library is used to ease the invocation of a function pointer. It converts the syntax from something that is abstruse and confusing to something that is easy to understand.

Wrapping a function invocation

Let's look at the following code in order to understand how to wrap a function invocation:

```cpp
/* uncalledbind.cpp */
#include <boost/bind.hpp>
#include <iostream>

void func() {
  std::cout << "Binding Function" << std::endl;
}

int main(void) {
  boost::bind(&func);
  return 0;
}
```

Save the preceding code as uncalledbind.cpp and then compile it using the following command:

g++ -Wall -ansi -I ../boost_1_58_0 uncalledbind.cpp -o uncalledbind

We will not get any line of text as output since we just created a function invocation but haven't actually called it. We have to add it to the () operator to call the function as follows:

```cpp
/* calledbind.cpp */
#include <boost/bind.hpp>
#include <iostream>

void func() {
  std::cout << "Binding Function" << std::endl;
}

int main(void) {
  boost::bind(&func)();
  return 0;
}
```

Name the preceding code calledbind.cpp and run the following command to compile it:

g++ -Wall -ansi -I ../boost_1_58_0 calledbind.cpp -o calledbind

Now, we will get the line of text as the output if we run the program, and of course, we will see the `bind()` function as an output:

```
boost::bind(&func)();
```

As we can see in the entire code, the change is only in one line, as shown in the preceding code snippet.

Now, let's use the function that has arguments to pass. We will use `boost::bind` for this purpose in the following code:

```
/* argumentbind.cpp */
#include <boost/bind.hpp>
#include <iostream>

void cubevolume(float f) {
   std::cout << "Volume of the cube is " << f * f * f << std::endl;
}

int main(void) {
   boost::bind(&cubevolume, 4.23f)();
   return 0;
}
```

Run the following command to compile the preceding `argumentbind.cpp` file:

```
g++ -Wall -ansi -I ../boost_1_58_0 argumentbind.cpp -o argumentbind
```

We successfully call the function with the argument using `boost::bind` because of which we obtain the following output:

```
Volume of the cube is 75.687
```

You need to remember that if the function has more than one argument, we have to match the function signature exactly. The following code will explain this in more detail:

```
/* signaturebind.cpp */
#include <boost/bind.hpp>
#include <iostream>
#include <string>

void identity(std::string name, int age, float height) {
   std::cout << "Name    : " << name << std::endl;
   std::cout << "Age     : " << age << " years old" << std::endl;
```

```
    std::cout << "Height : " << height << " inch" << std::endl;
}

int main(int argc, char * argv[]) {
  boost::bind(&identity, "John", 25, 68.89f)();
  return 0;
}
```

Compile the `signaturebind.cpp` code by using the following command:

g++ -Wall -ansi -I ../boost_1_58_0 signaturebind.cpp -o signaturebind

The signature of an identity function are `std::string`, `int`, and `float`. So, we have to fill the `bind` parameter with `std::string`, `int`, and `float`, respectively.

Because we have matched the function signature exactly, we will obtain an output as follows:

We have already been able to call the `global()` function in `boost::bind`. Now, let's continue to call the function inside a class in `boost::bind`. The code for this looks as follows:

```
/* classbind.cpp */
#include <boost/bind.hpp>
#include <iostream>
#include <string>

class TheClass {
public:
  void identity(std::string name, int age, float height) {
    std::cout << "Name    : " << name << std::endl;
    std::cout << "Age     : " << age << " years old" <<
    std::endl;
    std::cout << "Height : " << height << " inch" << std::endl;
  }
};
```

```
int main(void) {
  TheClass cls;
  boost::bind(&TheClass::identity, &cls, "John", 25, 68.89f)();
  return 0;
}
```

Compile the preceding `classbind.cpp` code by using following command:

g++ -Wall -ansi -I ../boost_1_58_0 classbind.cpp -o classbind

The output for this will be exactly the same as the `signaturebind.cpp` code since the content of the function is exactly the same as well:

boost::bind(&TheClass::identity, &cls, "John", 25, 68.89f)();

As we can see in the preceding code snippet, we have to pass the `boost:bind` arguments with the class and function name, object of the class, and parameter based on the function signature.

Working with the Boost.Bind library

So far, we have been able to use `boost::bind` for the global and class functions. However, when we use the `io_service` object with `boost::bind`, we will get a **non-copyable** error because the `io_service` object cannot be copied.

Now, let's take a look at `multithreads.cpp` again. We will modify the code to explain the use of `boost::bind` for the `io_service` object and we will still need the help of the `shared_ptr` pointer. Let's take a look at the following code snippet:

```
/* ioservicebind.cpp */
#include <boost/asio.hpp>
#include <boost/shared_ptr.hpp>
#include <boost/thread.hpp>
#include <boost/bind.hpp>
#include <iostream>

void WorkerThread(boost::shared_ptr<boost::asio::io_service>
iosvc, int counter) {
  std::cout << counter << ".\n";
  iosvc->run();
  std::cout << "End.\n";
}
```

```
int main(void) {
  boost::shared_ptr<boost::asio::io_service> io_svc(
    new boost::asio::io_service
  );

  boost::shared_ptr<boost::asio::io_service::work> worker(
    new boost::asio::io_service::work(*io_svc)
  );

  std::cout << "Press ENTER key to exit!" << std::endl;

  boost::thread_group threads;
  for(int i=1; i<=5; i++)
    threads.create_thread(boost::bind(&WorkerThread, io_svc, i));

  std::cin.get();

  io_svc->stop();

  threads.join_all();

  return 0;
}
```

We name the preceding code `ioservicebind.cpp` and compile it using the following command:

```
g++ -Wall -ansi -I ../boost_1_58_0 ioservicebind.cpp -o ioservicebind
-L ../boost_1_58_0/stage/lib -l boost_system-mgw49-mt-1_58 -l ws2_32
-l boost_thread-mgw49-mt-1_58
```

When we run `ioservicebind.exe`, we obtain the same output as `multithreads.exe`, but of course, the program will randomize the order of all threads:

```
boost::shared_ptr<boost::asio::io_service> io_svc(
  new boost::asio::io_service
);
```

We instantiate the `io_service` object in the `shared_ptr` pointer to make it **copyable** so that we can bind it to the worker `thread()` function that we use as a thread handler:

```
void WorkerThread(boost::shared_ptr<boost::asio::io_service>
iosvc, int counter)
```

The preceding code snippet shows us that the `io_service` object can be passed to the function. We do not need to define an `int` global variable as we did in the `multithreads.cpp` code snippet, since we can also pass the `int` argument to the `WorkerThread()` function:

```
std::cout << counter << ".\n";
```

Now, instead of incrementing the `int` variable to be shown to the user. We can use the preceding code snippet because we passed the counter from the `for` loop in the `main` block.

If we look at the `create_thread()` function, we see the different arguments that it gets in the `ioservicebind.cpp` and `multithreads.cpp` files. We can pass a pointer to the `void()` function that takes no arguments as the argument to the `create_thread()` function, as we can see in the `multithreads.cpp` file. We can also pass a binding function as an argument to the `create_thread()` function, as we can see in the `ioservicebind.cpp` file.

Synchronizing data access with the Boost. Mutex library

Have you ever got the following output when you ran the `multithreads.exe` or `ioservicebind.exe` executable files?

We can see in the preceding screenshot that there is a formatting issue here. Because the `std::cout` object is a global object, writing to it from different threads at once can cause output formatting issues. To solve this issue, we can use a `mutex` object that can be found in the `boost::mutex` object provided by the `thread` library. Mutex is used to synchronize access to any global data or shared data. To understand more about Mutex, take a look at the following code:

```cpp
/* mutexbind.cpp */
#include <boost/asio.hpp>
#include <boost/shared_ptr.hpp>
#include <boost/thread.hpp>
#include <boost/bind.hpp>
#include <iostream>

boost::mutex global_stream_lock;

void WorkerThread(boost::shared_ptr<boost::asio::io_service>
iosvc, int counter) {
  global_stream_lock.lock();
  std::cout << counter << ".\n";
  global_stream_lock.unlock();

  iosvc->run();

  global_stream_lock.lock();
  std::cout << "End.\n";
  global_stream_lock.unlock();
}

int main(void) {
  boost::shared_ptr<boost::asio::io_service> io_svc(
    new boost::asio::io_service
  );

  boost::shared_ptr<boost::asio::io_service::work> worker(
    new boost::asio::io_service::work(*io_svc)
  );

  std::cout << "Press ENTER key to exit!" << std::endl;

  boost::thread_group threads;
  for(int i=1; i<=5; i++)
    threads.create_thread(boost::bind(&WorkerThread, io_svc, i));

  std::cin.get();

  io_svc->stop();

  threads.join_all();

  return 0;
}
```

Save the preceding code as `mutexbind.cpp` and then compile it using the following command:

```
g++ -Wall -ansi -I ../boost_1_58_0 mutexbind.cpp -o mutexbind -L
../boost_1_58_0/stage/lib -l boost_system-mgw49-mt-1_58 -l ws2_32 -l
boost_thread-mgw49-mt-1_58
```

Now, run the `mutexbind.cpp` file and we will not face the formatting issue anymore:

```
boost::mutex global_stream_lock;
```

We instantiate the new `mutex` object, `global_stream_lock`. With this object, we can call the `lock()` and `unlock()` functions. The `lock()` function will block other threads that access the same function to wait for the current thread to be finished. The other threads can access the same function if only the current thread has called the `unlock()` function. One thing to remember is that we should not call the `lock()` function recursively because if the `lock()` function is not unlocked by the `unlock()` function, then thread deadlock will occur and it will freeze the application. So, we have to be careful when using the `lock()` and `unlock()` functions.

Giving some work to the I/O service

Now, it is time for us to give some work to the `io_service` object. Knowing more about `boost::bind` and `boost::mutex` will help us to give the `io_service` object work to do. There are two member functions in the `io_service` object: the `post()` and `dispatch()` functions, which we will frequently use to do this. The `post()` function is used to request the `io_service` object to run the `io_service` object's work after we queue up all the work, so it does not allow us to run the work immediately. While the `dispatch()` function is also used to make a request to the `io_service` object to run the `io_service` object's work, but it will execute the work right away without queuing it up.

Using the post() function

Let's examine the `post()` function by creating the following code. We will use the `mutexbind.cpp` file as our base code, since we will just modify the source code:

```
/* post.cpp */
#include <boost/asio.hpp>
#include <boost/shared_ptr.hpp>
#include <boost/thread.hpp>
#include <boost/bind.hpp>
```

```cpp
#include <iostream>

boost::mutex global_stream_lock;

void WorkerThread(boost::shared_ptr<boost::asio::io_service>
iosvc, int counter) {
  global_stream_lock.lock();
  std::cout << counter << ".\n";
  global_stream_lock.unlock();

  iosvc->run();

  global_stream_lock.lock();
  std::cout << "End.\n";
  global_stream_lock.unlock();
}

size_t fac(size_t n) {
  if ( n <= 1 ) {
    return n;
  }
  boost::this_thread::sleep(
    boost::posix_time::milliseconds(1000)
  );
  return n * fac(n - 1);
}

void CalculateFactorial(size_t n) {
  global_stream_lock.lock();
  std::cout << "Calculating " << n << "! factorial" << std::endl;
  global_stream_lock.unlock();

  size_t f = fac(n);

  global_stream_lock.lock();
  std::cout << n << "! = " << f << std::endl;
  global_stream_lock.unlock();
}

int main(void) {
  boost::shared_ptr<boost::asio::io_service> io_svc(
    new boost::asio::io_service
  );
```

```
boost::shared_ptr<boost::asio::io_service::work> worker(
    new boost::asio::io_service::work(*io_svc)
);

global_stream_lock.lock();
std::cout << "The program will exit once all work has finished."
<< std::endl;
global_stream_lock.unlock();

boost::thread_group threads;
for(int i=1; i<=5; i++)
    threads.create_thread(boost::bind(&WorkerThread, io_svc, i));

io_svc->post(boost::bind(CalculateFactorial, 5));
io_svc->post(boost::bind(CalculateFactorial, 6));
io_svc->post(boost::bind(CalculateFactorial, 7));

worker.reset();

threads.join_all();

return 0;
}
```

Name the preceding code as post.cpp and compile it using the following command:

```
g++ -Wall -ansi -I ../boost_1_58_0 post.cpp -o post -L
../boost_1_58_0/stage/lib -l boost_system-mgw49-mt-1_58 -l ws2_32 -l
boost_thread-mgw49-mt-1_58
```

Before we run the program, let's examine the code to understand its behavior:

```
size_t fac(size_t n) {
  if (n <= 1) {
    return n;
  }
  boost::this_thread::sleep(
    boost::posix_time::milliseconds(1000)
  );
  return n * fac(n - 1);
}
```

We add the `fac()` function to calculate the *n* factorial recursively. There is a time delay to slow down the process in order to see the work of our worker threads:

```
io_svc->post(boost::bind(CalculateFactorial, 5));
io_svc->post(boost::bind(CalculateFactorial, 6));
io_svc->post(boost::bind(CalculateFactorial, 7));
```

In the `main` block, we post three function objects on the `io_service` object, using the `post()` function. We do this just after we initialize the five worker threads. However, because we call the `run()` function of the `io_service` object inside each thread, the work of the `io_service` object will run. This means that the `post()` function will do its job.

Now, let's run `post.cpp` and take a look at what has happened here:

As we can see in the output of the preceding screenshot, the program runs the thread from the pool of threads, and after it finishes one thread, it calls the `post()` function from the `io_service` object until all three `post()` functions and all five threads have been called. Then, it calculates the factorial for each three *n* number. After it gets the `worker.reset()` function, it is notified that the work has been finished, and then it joins all the threads via the `threads.join_all()` function.

Using the dispatch() function

Now, let's examine the dispatch() function to give the io_service function some work. We will still use the mutexbind.cpp file as our base code and we will modify it a little so that it becomes like this:

```cpp
/* dispatch.cpp */
#include <boost/asio.hpp>
#include <boost/shared_ptr.hpp>
#include <boost/thread.hpp>
#include <boost/bind.hpp>
#include <iostream>

boost::mutex global_stream_lock;

void WorkerThread(boost::shared_ptr<boost::asio::io_service>
iosvc) {
  global_stream_lock.lock();
  std::cout << "Thread Start.\n";
  global_stream_lock.unlock();

  iosvc->run();

  global_stream_lock.lock();
  std::cout << "Thread Finish.\n";
  global_stream_lock.unlock();
}

void Dispatch(int i) {
  global_stream_lock.lock();
  std::cout << "dispath() Function for i = " << i <<  std::endl;
  global_stream_lock.unlock();
}

void Post(int i) {
  global_stream_lock.lock();
  std::cout << "post() Function for i = " << i <<  std::endl;
  global_stream_lock.unlock();
}
```

```cpp
void Running(boost::shared_ptr<boost::asio::io_service> iosvc) {
  for( int x = 0; x < 5; ++x ) {
    iosvc->dispatch(boost::bind(&Dispatch, x));
    iosvc->post(boost::bind(&Post, x));
    boost::this_thread::sleep(boost::posix_time::
    milliseconds(1000));
  }
}

int main(void) {
  boost::shared_ptr<boost::asio::io_service> io_svc(
    new boost::asio::io_service
  );

  boost::shared_ptr<boost::asio::io_service::work> worker(
    new boost::asio::io_service::work(*io_svc)
  );

  global_stream_lock.lock();
  std::cout << "The program will exit automatically once all work
  has finished." << std::endl;
  global_stream_lock.unlock();

  boost::thread_group threads;

  threads.create_thread(boost::bind(&WorkerThread, io_svc));

  io_svc->post(boost::bind(&Running, io_svc));

  worker.reset();

  threads.join_all();

  return 0;
}
```

Give the preceding code the name dispatch.cpp and compile it using the following command:

```
g++ -Wall -ansi -I ../boost_1_58_0 dispatch.cpp -o dispatch -L
../boost_1_58_0/stage/lib -l boost_system-mgw49-mt-1_58 -l ws2_32 -l
boost_thread-mgw49-mt-1_58
```

Now, let's run the program to get the following output:

```
C:\Windows\system32\cmd.exe

C:\CPP>g++ -Wall -ansi -I ../boost_1_58_0 dispatch.cpp -o dispatch -L ../boost_1
_58_0/stage/lib -l boost_system-mgw49-mt-1_58 -l ws2_32 -l boost_thread-mgw49-mt
-1_58

C:\CPP>dispatch
The program will exit automatically once all work has finished.
Thread Start.
dispath() Function for i = 0
dispath() Function for i = 1
dispath() Function for i = 2
dispath() Function for i = 3
dispath() Function for i = 4
post() Function for i = 0
post() Function for i = 1
post() Function for i = 2
post() Function for i = 3
post() Function for i = 4
Thread Finish.

C:\CPP>
```

Different than the `post.cpp` file, in the `dispatch.cpp` file, we just create one worker thread. Also, we add two functions, `dispatch()`, and `post()` to understand the difference between both functions:

```
iosvc->dispatch(boost::bind(&Dispatch, x));
iosvc->post(boost::bind(&Post, x));
```

If we look at the preceding code snippet inside the `Running()` function, we expect to get the ordered output between the `dispatch()` and `post()` functions. However, when we see the output, we find that the result is different because the `dispatch()` function is called first and the `post()` function is called after it. This happens because the `dispatch()` function can be invoked from the current worker thread, while the `post()` function has to wait until the handler of the worker is complete before it can be invoked. In other words, the `dispatch()` function's events can be executed from the current worker thread even if there are other pending events queued up, while the `post()` function's events have to wait until the handler completes the execution before being allowed to be executed.

Summary

There are two functions that we can use to get the io_service object working for us: the run() and poll() member functions. The run() function blocks the program because it has to wait for the work that we assign to it, while the poll() function does not block the program. When we need to give some work to the io_service object, we simply use the poll() or run() functions, depending on what we need, and then we call the post() or dispatch() functions as needed. The post() function is used to command the io_service object in order to run the given handler, but without permitting the handler is called by the io_service object from inside this function. While the dispatch() function is used to call the handler in the thread in which the run() or poll() functions are currently being invoked. The fundamental difference between the dispatch() and the post() functions is that the dispatch() function completes the work right away whenever it can, while the post() function always queues the work.

We found out about the io_service object, how to run it, and how to give it some work. Now, let's move to the next chapter to find out more about the Boost.Asio library, and we will be one step closer to creating our network programming.

5
Delving into the Boost.Asio Library

Now that we are able to run the `io_service` object and give it some work to do, it is time for us to find out more about other objects in the `Boost.Asio` library in order to develop the network application. All works of the `io_service` object we used before are run asynchronously but not in a serialized order, which means we are not able to determine the order of the `io_service` object's work that will be run. Also, we have to consider what we will do if our application encounters any errors at runtime and think about time interval in running any `io_service` object work. Therefore, in this chapter, we will discuss the following topics:

- Serially executing the work of the `io_service` object
- Catching the exception(s) and handling them properly
- Executing the work in the desired amount of time

Serializing the I/O service work

Suppose we want to queue up the work to be done but the order is important. If we just apply the asynchronous method, we won't know the order of work we will get. We need to make sure that the order of work is the one we want and have designed it to be. For instance, if we post Work A, Work B, and Work C, in that order, we want to keep that order at runtime.

Using the strand function

Strand is a class in the `io_service` object that provides handler execution serialization. It can be used to ensure the work we have will be executed serially. Let us examine the following code to understand serializing by using the `strand` function. But first, we will start without using the `strand()` and `lock()` functions:

```cpp
/* nonstrand.cpp */
#include <boost/asio.hpp>
#include <boost/shared_ptr.hpp>
#include <boost/thread.hpp>
#include <boost/thread/mutex.hpp>
#include <boost/bind.hpp>
#include <iostream>

boost::mutex global_stream_lock;

void WorkerThread(boost::shared_ptr<boost::asio::io_service>
iosvc, int counter) {
  global_stream_lock.lock();
  std::cout << "Thread " << counter << " Start.\n";
  global_stream_lock.unlock();

  iosvc->run();

  global_stream_lock.lock();
  std::cout << "Thread " << counter << " End.\n";
global_stream_lock.unlock();
}

void Print(int number) {
  std::cout << "Number: " << number << std::endl;
}

int main(void) {
  boost::shared_ptr<boost::asio::io_service> io_svc(
    new boost::asio::io_service
  );
```

```
boost::shared_ptr<boost::asio::io_service::work> worker(
  new boost::asio::io_service::work(*io_svc)
);

global_stream_lock.lock();
std::cout << "The program will exit once all work has
finished.\n";
global_stream_lock.unlock();

boost::thread_group threads;
for(int i=1; i<=5; i++)
  threads.create_thread(boost::bind(&WorkerThread, io_svc, i));

boost::this_thread::sleep(boost::posix_time::milliseconds(500));

io_svc->post(boost::bind(&Print, 1));
io_svc->post(boost::bind(&Print, 2));
io_svc->post(boost::bind(&Print, 3));
io_svc->post(boost::bind(&Print, 4));
io_svc->post(boost::bind(&Print, 5));

worker.reset();

threads.join_all();

return 0;
}
```

Save the preceding code as nonstrand.cpp and compile it with the following command:

```
g++ -Wall -ansi -I ../boost_1_58_0 nonstrand.cpp -o nonstrand -L
../boost_1_58_0/stage/lib -l boost_system-mgw49-mt-1_58 -l ws2_32 -l
libboost_thread-mgw49-mt-1_58
```

Then, run it by typing `nonstrand` in the console window. We will get an output similar to the following:

You may get a different output, and running the program several times does, in fact, yield different orders of the results. This is because, as we discussed in the previous chapter, without the `lock` object, the output will be unsynchronized, shown as follows. We can notice that the result looks disordered:

Number: Number: 1

Number: 5

Number: 3

2

Number: 4

As we can see in the following snippet, we do not use the `lock` object to synchronize the output. This is why we get the output as shown in the preceding screenshot.

```cpp
void Print(int number) {
  std::cout << "Number: " << number << std::endl;
}
```

Now, let us apply the `strand` function to synchronize the flow of the program. Type the following code and save it as `strand.cpp`:

```cpp
/* strand.cpp */
#include <boost/asio.hpp>
#include <boost/shared_ptr.hpp>
#include <boost/thread.hpp>
#include <boost/thread/mutex.hpp>
#include <boost/bind.hpp>
#include <iostream>

boost::mutex global_stream_lock;

void WorkerThread(boost::shared_ptr<boost::asio::io_service>
iosvc, int counter) {
  global_stream_lock.lock();
  std::cout << "Thread " << counter << " Start.\n";
  global_stream_lock.unlock();

  iosvc->run();

  global_stream_lock.lock();
  std::cout << "Thread " << counter << " End.\n";
  global_stream_lock.unlock();
}

void Print(int number) {
  std::cout << "Number: " << number << std::endl;
}

int main(void) {
  boost::shared_ptr<boost::asio::io_service> io_svc(
    new boost::asio::io_service
  );

  boost::shared_ptr<boost::asio::io_service::work> worker(
    new boost::asio::io_service::work(*io_svc)
  );

  boost::asio::io_service::strand strand(*io_svc);
```

```
    global_stream_lock.lock();
    std::cout << "The program will exit once all work has
    finished.\n";
    global_stream_lock.unlock();

    boost::thread_group threads;
    for(int i=1; i<=5; i++)
      threads.create_thread(boost::bind(&WorkerThread, io_svc, i));

    boost::this_thread::sleep(boost::posix_time::milliseconds(500));

    strand.post(boost::bind(&Print, 1));
    strand.post(boost::bind(&Print, 2));
    strand.post(boost::bind(&Print, 3));
    strand.post(boost::bind(&Print, 4));
    strand.post(boost::bind(&Print, 5));

    worker.reset();

    threads.join_all();

    return 0;
  }
```

Compile the preceding code by using the following command:

```
g++ -Wall -ansi -I ../boost_1_58_0 strand.cpp -o strand -L
../boost_1_58_0/stage/lib -l boost_system-mgw49-mt-1_58 -l ws2_32 -l
libboost_thread-mgw49-mt-1_58
```

We make just a little modification from nonstrand.cpp to strand.cpp, but the impact is big. Before we run the program, let us distinguish the code between nonstrand.cpp and strand.cpp:

```
  io_svc->post(boost::bind(&Print, 1));
  io_svc->post(boost::bind(&Print, 2));
  io_svc->post(boost::bind(&Print, 3));
  io_svc->post(boost::bind(&Print, 4));
  io_svc->post(boost::bind(&Print, 5));
```

We use the `post()` function in the `io_service` object to give it work. But by using this method, the flow of the program is unpredictable because it is not synchronized:

```
strand.post(boost::bind(&Print, 1));
strand.post(boost::bind(&Print, 2));
strand.post(boost::bind(&Print, 3));
strand.post(boost::bind(&Print, 4));
strand.post(boost::bind(&Print, 5));
```

Then, we use the `strand` object to give the work to the `io_service` object. By using this method, we will ensure that the order of the work is exactly the same as what we have stated in the code. To prove it, let's take a look at the following output:

The order of the work is the same as the sequence of the work in our code. We are shown the output of the work in numerical order, which is:

Number: 1

Number: 2

Number: 3

Number: 4

Number: 5

And, if you remember, we continue to omit the `lock()` function from the `Print()` function and it still runs properly due to the `strand` object's usage. Now, no matter how many times we re-run the program, the results are always in ascending order.

Wrapping a handler through the strand object

There is a function in `boost::asio::strand` called the `wrap()` method. Based on the official Boost documentation, it creates a new handler function object that will automatically pass the wrapped handler to the `strand` object's dispatch function when it is called. Let us look at the following code to explain it:

```cpp
/* strandwrap.cpp */
#include <boost/asio.hpp>
#include <boost/shared_ptr.hpp>
#include <boost/thread.hpp>
#include <boost/thread/mutex.hpp>
#include <boost/bind.hpp>
#include <iostream>

boost::mutex global_stream_lock;

void WorkerThread(boost::shared_ptr<boost::asio::io_service>
iosvc, int counter) {
  global_stream_lock.lock();
  std::cout << "Thread " << counter << " Start.\n";
  global_stream_lock.unlock();

  iosvc->run();

  global_stream_lock.lock();
  std::cout << "Thread " << counter << " End.\n";
  global_stream_lock.unlock();
}

void Print(int number) {
  std::cout << "Number: " << number << std::endl;
}

int main(void) {
  boost::shared_ptr<boost::asio::io_service> io_svc(
    new boost::asio::io_service
  );
```

```
boost::shared_ptr<boost::asio::io_service::work> worker(
    new boost::asio::io_service::work(*io_svc)
);

boost::asio::io_service::strand strand(*io_svc);

global_stream_lock.lock();
std::cout << "The program will exit once all work has finished."
<<   std::endl;
global_stream_lock.unlock();

boost::thread_group threads;
for(int i=1; i<=5; i++)
    threads.create_thread(boost::bind(&WorkerThread, io_svc, i));

boost::this_thread::sleep(boost::posix_time::milliseconds(100));
io_svc->post(strand.wrap(boost::bind(&Print, 1)));
io_svc->post(strand.wrap(boost::bind(&Print, 2)));

boost::this_thread::sleep(boost::posix_time::milliseconds(100));
io_svc->post(strand.wrap(boost::bind(&Print, 3)));
io_svc->post(strand.wrap(boost::bind(&Print, 4)));

boost::this_thread::sleep(boost::posix_time::milliseconds(100));
io_svc->post(strand.wrap(boost::bind(&Print, 5)));
io_svc->post(strand.wrap(boost::bind(&Print, 6)));

worker.reset();

threads.join_all();

return 0;
}
```

Give the preceding code the name strandwrap.cpp, then compile it by using the following command:

```
g++ -Wall -ansi -I ../boost_1_58_0 strandwrap.cpp -o strandwrap -L
../boost_1_58_0/stage/lib -l boost_system-mgw49-mt-1_58 -l ws2_32 -l
libboost_thread-mgw49-mt-1_58
```

Now, run the program and we will get the following output:

```
C:\CPP>g++ -Wall -ansi -I ../boost_1_58_0 strandwrap.cpp -o strandwrap -L ../boo
st_1_58_0/stage/lib -l boost_system-mgw49-mt-1_58 -l ws2_32 -l libboost_thread-m
gw49-mt-1_58

C:\CPP>strandwrap
The program will exit once all work has finished.
Thread 2 Start.
Thread 3 Start.
Thread 4 Start.
Thread 5 Start.
Thread 1 Start.
Number: 1
Number: 2
Number: 3
Number: 4
Number: 5
Number: 6
Thread 1 End.
Thread 5 End.
Thread 4 End.
Thread 3 End.
Thread 2 End.

C:\CPP>
```

However, if we run the program many times, it might produce a random output like the following:

Number: 2

Number: 1

Number: 3

Number: 4

Number: 6

Number: 5

Although the work is guaranteed to be executed serially, it is not guaranteed which work's order actually takes place as a result of the built-in handler wrapper. And if the order is really important, we have to look at the built-in handler wrapper itself when using the strand object.

Handling exceptions and errors

Sometimes, our code will throw an exception or error at runtime. As you may remember in our discussion of the lexical.cpp in *Chapter 3, Introducing the Boost C++ Libraries*, we must sometimes use exception handling in our code, and we will now dig it up to delve into exception and error handling.

Handling an exception

An exception is a way of reacting to a situation in which the code has exceptional circumstances by transferring control to the handler. To handle the exception, we need to use the `try-catch` block in our code; then, if an exceptional circumstance arises, an exception will be thrown to the exception handler.

Now, take a look at the following code to see how exception handling is used:

```cpp
/* exception.cpp */
#include <boost/asio.hpp>
#include <boost/shared_ptr.hpp>
#include <boost/thread.hpp>
#include <boost/thread/mutex.hpp>
#include <boost/bind.hpp>
#include <iostream>

boost::mutex global_stream_lock;

void WorkerThread(boost::shared_ptr<boost::asio::io_service>
iosvc, int counter) {
  global_stream_lock.lock();
  std::cout << "Thread " << counter << " Start.\n";
  global_stream_lock.unlock();

  try {
    iosvc->run();

    global_stream_lock.lock();
    std::cout << "Thread " << counter << " End.\n";
    global_stream_lock.unlock();
  }
  catch(std::exception & ex) {
    global_stream_lock.lock();
    std::cout << "Message: " << ex.what() << ".\n";
    global_stream_lock.unlock();
  }
}

void ThrowAnException(boost::shared_ptr<boost::asio::io_service>
iosvc, int counter) {
  global_stream_lock.lock();
  std::cout << "Throw Exception " << counter << "\n" ;
  global_stream_lock.unlock();
```

```
      throw(std::runtime_error("The Exception !!!"));
}

int main(void) {
  boost::shared_ptr<boost::asio::io_service> io_svc(
    new boost::asio::io_service
  );

  boost::shared_ptr<boost::asio::io_service::work> worker(
    new boost::asio::io_service::work(*io_svc)
  );

  global_stream_lock.lock();
  std::cout << "The program will exit once all work has
  finished.\n";
  global_stream_lock.unlock();

  boost::thread_group threads;
  for(int i=1; i<=2; i++)
    threads.create_thread(boost::bind(&WorkerThread, io_svc, i));

  io_svc->post(boost::bind(&ThrowAnException, io_svc, 1));
  io_svc->post(boost::bind(&ThrowAnException, io_svc, 2));
  io_svc->post(boost::bind(&ThrowAnException, io_svc, 3));
  io_svc->post(boost::bind(&ThrowAnException, io_svc, 4));
  io_svc->post(boost::bind(&ThrowAnException, io_svc, 5));

  threads.join_all();

  return 0;
}
```

Save the preceding code as exception.cpp and run the following command to
compile it:

```
g++ -Wall -ansi -I ../boost_1_58_0 exception.cpp -o exception -L
../boost_1_58_0/stage/lib -l boost_system-mgw49-mt-1_58 -l ws2_32 -l
libboost_thread-mgw49-mt-1_58
```

Then, run the program and you should get the following output:

As we can see, we are not shown the line from `std::cout << "Thread " <<`
`counter << " End.\n";` because of the exception. When the work of the
`io_service` object is run, it always throws an exception by using the `throw`
keyword so that the exception will be caught by the `catch` block within the
`WorkerThread` function, since the `iosvc->run()` function is inside the `try` block.

We can also see that although we post work for the `io_service` object five times, the
exception handling only handle two exceptions because once the thread has finished,
the `join_all()` function in the thread will finish the thread and exit the program. In
other words, we can say that once the exception is handled, the thread exits to join
the call. Additional code that might have thrown an exception will never be called.

How about if we put in the `io_service` object's work invocation recursively? Will
it lead to an infinitely running program? Let us try to throw the exception infinitely.
The code will look like the following:

```cpp
/* exception2.cpp */
#include <boost/asio.hpp>
#include <boost/shared_ptr.hpp>
#include <boost/thread.hpp>
#include <boost/thread/mutex.hpp>
#include <boost/bind.hpp>
#include <iostream>

boost::mutex global_stream_lock;
```

```
void WorkerThread(boost::shared_ptr<boost::asio::io_service>
iosvc, int counter) {
  global_stream_lock.lock();
  std::cout << "Thread " << counter << " Start.\n";
  global_stream_lock.unlock();

  try {
    iosvc->run();

    global_stream_lock.lock();
    std::cout << "Thread " << counter << " End.\n";
    global_stream_lock.unlock();
  }
  catch(std::exception &ex) {
    global_stream_lock.lock();
    std::cout << "Message: " << ex.what() << ".\n";
    global_stream_lock.unlock();
  }
}

void ThrowAnException(boost::shared_ptr<boost::asio::io_service>
iosvc) {
  global_stream_lock.lock();
  std::cout << "Throw Exception\n" ;
  global_stream_lock.unlock();

  iosvc->post(boost::bind(&ThrowAnException, iosvc));

  throw(std::runtime_error("The Exception !!!"));
}

int main(void) {
  boost::shared_ptr<boost::asio::io_service> io_svc(
    new boost::asio::io_service
  );

  boost::shared_ptr<boost::asio::io_service::work> worker(
    new boost::asio::io_service::work(*io_svc)
  );

  global_stream_lock.lock();
  std::cout << "The program will exit once all work has
finished.\n";
  global_stream_lock.unlock();
```

```
boost::thread_group threads;
for(int i=1; i<=5; i++)
    threads.create_thread(boost::bind(&WorkerThread, io_svc, i));

io_svc->post(boost::bind(&ThrowAnException, io_svc));

threads.join_all();

return 0;
}
```

Save the preceding code as exception2.cpp and compile it by using the following command:

```
g++ -Wall -ansi -I ../boost_1_58_0 exception2.cpp -o exception2 -L
../boost_1_58_0/stage/lib -l boost_system-mgw49-mt-1_58 -l ws2_32 -l
libboost_thread-mgw49-mt-1_58
```

Now, let us examine the code:

```
iosvc->post(boost::bind(&ThrowAnException, iosvc));
```

We add the preceding code snippet inside the ThrowAnException function. Every time the ThrowAnException function is called, it will call itself. Then, it should be an infinite program since there is a recursive function. Let us run the program to prove this by typing the exception2 command in the console window. The output will be like the following:

Fortunately, the program was able to finish successfully. This happened because the exception propagated through the run() function and the worker threads exited. After that, all the threads finished and the join_all() function was called. That is why the program exits even though there is still work left in the io_service object.

Handling an error

In our previous example, we used the run() function without any parameters, but in fact, the function has two overload methods, std::size_t run() and std::size_t run(boost::system::error_code & ec). The latter method has an error code parameter that will be set if an error occurs.

Now, let us try to use an error code as an input parameter in the run() function. Take a look at the following code:

```cpp
/* errorcode.cpp */
#include <boost/asio.hpp>
#include <boost/shared_ptr.hpp>
#include <boost/thread.hpp>
#include <boost/thread/mutex.hpp>
#include <boost/bind.hpp>
#include <iostream>

boost::mutex global_stream_lock;

void WorkerThread(boost::shared_ptr<boost::asio::io_service>
iosvc, int counter) {
  global_stream_lock.lock();
  std::cout << "Thread " << counter << " Start.\n";
  global_stream_lock.unlock();

  boost::system::error_code ec;
  iosvc->run(ec);

  if(ec) {
    global_stream_lock.lock();
    std::cout << "Message: " << ec << ".\n";
    global_stream_lock.unlock();
  }
```

```
  global_stream_lock.lock();
  std::cout << "Thread " << counter << " End.\n";
  global_stream_lock.unlock();
}

void ThrowAnException(boost::shared_ptr<boost::asio::io_service>
iosvc) {
  global_stream_lock.lock();
  std::cout << "Throw Exception\n" ;
  global_stream_lock.unlock();

  iosvc->post(boost::bind(&ThrowAnException, iosvc));

  throw(std::runtime_error("The Exception !!!"));
}

int main(void) {
  boost::shared_ptr<boost::asio::io_service> io_svc(
    new boost::asio::io_service
  );

  boost::shared_ptr<boost::asio::io_service::work> worker(
    new boost::asio::io_service::work(*io_svc)
  );

  global_stream_lock.lock();
  std::cout << "The program will exit once all work has
  finished.\n";
  global_stream_lock.unlock();

  boost::thread_group threads;
  for(int i=1; i<=5; i++)
    threads.create_thread(boost::bind(&WorkerThread, io_svc, i));

  io_svc->post(boost::bind(&ThrowAnException, io_svc));

  threads.join_all();

  return 0;
}
```

Save the preceding code as `errorcode.cpp` and use the following command to compile the code:

```
g++ -Wall -ansi -I ../boost_1_58_0 errorcode.cpp -o errorcode -L ../
boost_1_58_0/stage/lib -l boost_system-mgw49-mt-1_58 -l ws2_32 -l
libboost_thread-mgw49-mt-1_58
```

Now, run the program by typing the `errorcode` command in the console. As a result of doing so, the program will crash. The following screenshot shows the output:

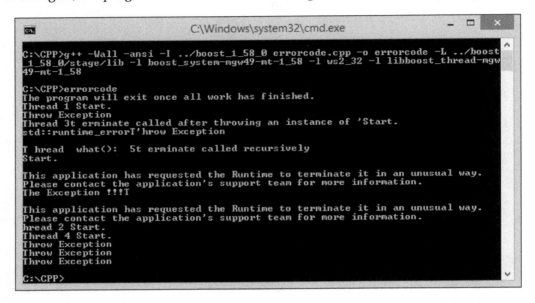

We intend to retrieve the error code by using the following code:

```
iosvc->run(ec);
```

And we can catch the error by using the `if` block, as follows:

```
if(ec)
```

However, in error variable approach, user exceptions translate to `boost::asio` exceptions; thus, the error variable `ec` does not interpret the user exception as an error so the exception is not caught by the handler. If the `Boost.Asio` library needs to throw an error, it will become an exception if there is no error variable, or it will be converted into an error variable. It is better if we keep using the `try-catch` block to catch any exceptions or errors.

Also, we have to examine the type of exception, which is either system failure or context failure. If it is system failure, then we have to invoke the `stop()` function in the `io_service` class to ensure the work object has been destroyed in order for the program to be able to exit. In contrast, if the exception is context failure, we need the worker thread to call the `run()` function once more in order to prevent the thread from dying. Now, take a look at the following code to understand the concept:

```cpp
/* errorcode2.cpp */
#include <boost/asio.hpp>
#include <boost/shared_ptr.hpp>
#include <boost/thread.hpp>
#include <boost/thread/mutex.hpp>
#include <boost/bind.hpp>
#include <iostream>

boost::mutex global_stream_lock;

void WorkerThread(boost::shared_ptr<boost::asio::io_service>
iosvc, int counter) {
  global_stream_lock.lock();
  std::cout << "Thread " << counter << " Start.\n";
  global_stream_lock.unlock();

  while(true) {
    try {
      boost::system::error_code ec;
      iosvc->run(ec);
      if(ec) {
        global_stream_lock.lock();
        std::cout << "Error Message: " << ec << ".\n";
        global_stream_lock.unlock();
      }
      break;
    }
    catch(std::exception &ex) {
      global_stream_lock.lock();
      std::cout << "Exception Message: " << ex.what() << ".\n";
      global_stream_lock.unlock();
    }
  }
}
```

```
    global_stream_lock.lock();
    std::cout << "Thread " << counter << " End.\n";
    global_stream_lock.unlock();
}

void ThrowAnException(boost::shared_ptr<boost::asio::io_service>
iosvc) {
  global_stream_lock.lock();
  std::cout << "Throw Exception\n" ;
  global_stream_lock.unlock();

  iosvc->post(boost::bind(&ThrowAnException, iosvc));

  throw(std::runtime_error("The Exception !!!"));
}

int main(void) {
  boost::shared_ptr<boost::asio::io_service> io_svc(
    new boost::asio::io_service
  );

  boost::shared_ptr<boost::asio::io_service::work> worker(
    new boost::asio::io_service::work(*io_svc)
  );

  global_stream_lock.lock();
  std::cout << "The program will exit once all work has
  finished.\n";
  global_stream_lock.unlock();

  boost::thread_group threads;
  for(int i=1; i<=5; i++)
    threads.create_thread(boost::bind(&WorkerThread, io_svc, i));

  io_svc->post(boost::bind(&ThrowAnException, io_svc));

  threads.join_all();

  return 0;
}
```

Save the preceding code as `errorcode2.cpp` and then compile it by executing the following command:

```
g++ -Wall -ansi -I ../boost_1_58_0 errorcode2.cpp -o errorcode2 -L
../boost_1_58_0/stage/lib -l boost_system-mgw49-mt-1_58 -l ws2_32 -l
libboost_thread-mgw49-mt-1_58
```

If we run the program, we will see that it will not exit, and we have to press *Ctrl* + *C* to stop the program:

```
C:\Windows\system32\cmd.exe                                 _ □ ×
Throw Exception
Exception Message: The Exception !!!.
Throw Exception
Exception Message: The Exception !!!.
Throw Exception
Exception Message: The Exception !!!.
Throw Exception
Exception Message: The Exception !!!.
Throw Exception
Exception Message: The Exception !!!.
Throw Exception
Exception Message: The Exception !!!.
Throw Exception
Exception Message: The Exception !!!.
Throw Exception
Exception Message: The Exception !!!.
Throw Exception
Exception Message: ^C
C:\CPP>
```

If we see the following code snippet:

```
while(true) {
    try {
        . . .
        iosvc->run(ec);
        if(ec)
        . . .
    }
    catch(std::exception &ex) {
        . . .
    }
}
```

The worker thread is looping. This is also the case when an exception occurs in the output result (indicated by the `Throw Exception` and the `Exception Message: The Exception!!!` output). Call the `run()` function again so it will post a new event to the queue. Of course, we don't want this situation to occur in our application.

Timing the work execution using the timer class

There is a class in the Boost C++ library that provides the ability to conduct a blocking or asynchronous wait for a timer until it expires, known as the **deadline timer**. A deadline timer indicates one of two states: expired or not expired.

An expiring timer

Here, we are going to create a timer that will expire in 10 seconds. Let us take a look at the following code:

```
/* timer.cpp */
#include <boost/asio.hpp>
#include <boost/shared_ptr.hpp>
#include <boost/thread.hpp>
#include <boost/thread/mutex.hpp>
#include <boost/bind.hpp>
#include <iostream>

boost::mutex global_stream_lock;

void WorkerThread(boost::shared_ptr<boost::asio::io_service> iosvc,
int counter) {
  global_stream_lock.lock();
  std::cout << "Thread " << counter << " Start.\n";
  global_stream_lock.unlock();

  while(true) {
    try {
      boost::system::error_code ec;
      iosvc->run(ec);
      if(ec) {
        global_stream_lock.lock();
        std::cout << "Message: " << ec << ".\n";
        global_stream_lock.unlock();
      }
      break;
    }
    catch(std::exception &ex) {
      global_stream_lock.lock();
```

```
          std::cout << "Message: " << ex.what() << ".\n";
          global_stream_lock.unlock();
      }
  }

  global_stream_lock.lock();
  std::cout << "Thread " << counter << " End.\n";
  global_stream_lock.unlock();
}

void TimerHandler(const boost::system::error_code & ec) {
  if(ec) {
    global_stream_lock.lock();
    std::cout << "Error Message: " << ec << ".\n";
    global_stream_lock.unlock();
  }
  else {
    global_stream_lock.lock();
    std::cout << "You see this line because you have waited for 10
    seconds.\n";
    std::cout << "Now press ENTER to exit.\n";
    global_stream_lock.unlock();
  }
}

int main(void) {
  boost::shared_ptr<boost::asio::io_service> io_svc(
    new boost::asio::io_service
  );

  boost::shared_ptr<boost::asio::io_service::work> worker(
    new boost::asio::io_service::work(*io_svc)
  );

  global_stream_lock.lock();
  std::cout << "Wait for ten seconds to see what happen, ";
  std::cout << "otherwise press ENTER to exit!\n";
  global_stream_lock.unlock();

  boost::thread_group threads;
  for(int i=1; i<=5; i++)
    threads.create_thread(boost::bind(&WorkerThread, io_svc, i));
```

```
boost::asio::deadline_timer timer(*io_svc);
timer.expires_from_now(boost::posix_time::seconds(10));
timer.async_wait(TimerHandler);

std::cin.get();

io_svc->stop();

threads.join_all();

return 0;
}
```

Save the preceding code as `timer.cpp` and run the following command to compile it:

```
g++ -Wall -ansi -I ../boost_1_58_0 timer.cpp -o timer -L
../boost_1_58_0/stage/lib -l boost_system-mgw49-mt-1_58 -l ws2_32 -l
libboost_thread-mgw49-mt-1_58
```

Now, let us distinguish the code before we run it:

```
boost::asio::deadline_timer timer(*io_svc);
timer.expires_from_now(boost::posix_time::seconds(10));
timer.async_wait(TimerHandler);
```

Before the program calls the `TimerHandler` function, it has to wait for 10 seconds because we use the `expires_from_now` function from the `timer` object. The `async_wait()` function will wait until the timer has expired:

```
void TimerHandler(const boost::system::error_code & ec) {
  if(ec)
  . . .
}
else {
  global_stream_lock.lock();
  std::cout << "You see this line because you have waited for 10
  seconds.\n";
  std::cout << "Now press ENTER to exit.\n";
  global_stream_lock.unlock();
}
```

After the timer has expired, the `TimerHandler` function will be invoked and since there is no error, the program will execute the code inside the `else` block. Let us run the program to see the complete output:

And, since we used the `async_wait()` function, we can hit the *Enter* key to exit the program before we see the line, **Now press ENTER to exit**.

Using the timer along with the boost::bind function

Let us try to create a recurring timer. We have to initialize the global timer object in order for the object to become a shared object. To achieve this, we need help from the `shared_ptr` pointer and the `boost::bind` method to make and keep the thread safe since we will use a shared object:

```
/* timer2.cpp */
#include <boost/asio.hpp>
#include <boost/shared_ptr.hpp>
#include <boost/thread.hpp>
#include <boost/thread/mutex.hpp>
#include <boost/bind.hpp>
#include <iostream>

boost::mutex global_stream_lock;

void WorkerThread(boost::shared_ptr<boost::asio::io_service>
iosvc, int counter) {
  global_stream_lock.lock();
  std::cout << "Thread " << counter << " Start.\n";
  global_stream_lock.unlock();
```

```
        while( true ) {
          try {
            boost::system::error_code ec;
            iosvc->run(ec);
            if(ec) {
              global_stream_lock.lock();
              std::cout << "Message: " << ec << ".\n";
              global_stream_lock.unlock();
            }
            break;
          }
          catch(std::exception &ex) {
            global_stream_lock.lock();
            std::cout << "Message: " << ex.what() << ".\n";
            global_stream_lock.unlock();
          }
        }

        global_stream_lock.lock();
        std::cout << "Thread " << counter << " End.\n";
        global_stream_lock.unlock();
      }

      void TimerHandler(
        const boost::system::error_code &ec,
        boost::shared_ptr<boost::asio::deadline_timer> tmr
      )
      {
        if(ec) {
          global_stream_lock.lock();
          std::cout << "Error Message: " << ec << ".\n";
          global_stream_lock.unlock();
        }
        else {
          global_stream_lock.lock();
          std::cout << "You see this every three seconds.\n";
          global_stream_lock.unlock();

          tmr->expires_from_now( boost::posix_time::seconds(3));
          tmr->async_wait(boost::bind(&TimerHandler, _1, tmr));
        }
      }
```

```
int main(void) {
  boost::shared_ptr<boost::asio::io_service> io_svc(
    new boost::asio::io_service
  );

  boost::shared_ptr<boost::asio::io_service::work> worker(
    new boost::asio::io_service::work(*io_svc)
  );

  global_stream_lock.lock();
  std::cout << "Press ENTER to exit!\n";
  global_stream_lock.unlock();

  boost::thread_group threads;
  for(int i=1; i<=5; i++)
    threads.create_thread(boost::bind(&WorkerThread, io_svc, i));

  boost::shared_ptr<boost::asio::deadline_timer> timer(
    new boost::asio::deadline_timer(*io_svc)
  );
  timer->expires_from_now( boost::posix_time::seconds(3));
  timer->async_wait(boost::bind(&TimerHandler, _1, timer));

  std::cin.get();

  io_svc->stop();

  threads.join_all();

  return 0;
}
```

Save the preceding code as `timer2.cpp` and run the following command to compile it:

```
g++ -Wall -ansi -I ../boost_1_58_0 timer2.cpp -o timer2 -L
../boost_1_58_0/stage/lib -l boost_system-mgw49-mt-1_58 -l ws2_32 -l
libboost_thread-mgw49-mt-1_58
```

Now, run the program. We will get a recurring output, which we can stop by hitting the *Enter* key, as follows:

```
C:\Windows\system32\cmd.exe

C:\CPP>g++ -Wall -ansi -I ../boost_1_58_0 timer2.cpp -o timer2 -L ../boost_1_58_
0/stage/lib -l boost_system-mgw49-mt-1_58 -l ws2_32 -l libboost_thread-mgw49-mt-
1_58

C:\CPP>timer2
Press ENTER to exit!
Thread 1 Start.
Thread 2 Start.
Thread 3 Start.
Thread 4 Start.
Thread 5 Start.
You see this every three seconds.
You see this every three seconds.
You see this every three seconds.
You see this every three seconds.
You see this every three seconds.
You see this every three seconds.

Thread 5 End.
Thread 4 End.
Thread 3 End.
```

We see from the output that the timer is ticked every three seconds and the work will be stopped after the user presses the *Enter* key. Now, let us see the following code snippet:

```
timer->async_wait(boost::bind(&TimerHandler, _1, timer));
```

The `boost::bind` function helps us to use the global timer object. And if we look deeper, we can use the `_1` parameter for our `boost::bind` function. If we read the documentation of the `boost::bind` function, we will find that the `_1` parameter is a placeholder argument that will be substituted by the first input argument.

> For more information about binding with a placeholder, check out the official Boost documentation at www.boost.org/doc/libs/1_58_0/libs/bind/doc/html/bind.html.
>
> And for more information on placeholder arguments, see en.cppreference.com/w/cpp/utility/functional/placeholders.

Using the timer along with the boost::strand function

Since the timer is asynchronously executed, it is possible that the timer execution is not in a serialized process. The timer might be executed in one thread while another event is executed at the same time. As we have discussed previously, we can utilize the strand function to serialize the order of execution. Let us take a look at the following code snippet:

```cpp
/* timer3.cpp */
#include <boost/asio.hpp>
#include <boost/shared_ptr.hpp>
#include <boost/thread.hpp>
#include <boost/thread/mutex.hpp>
#include <boost/bind.hpp>
#include <iostream>

boost::mutex global_stream_lock;

void WorkerThread(boost::shared_ptr<boost::asio::io_service>
iosvc, int counter) {
  global_stream_lock.lock();
  std::cout << "Thread " << counter << " Start.\n";
  global_stream_lock.unlock();

  while( true ) {
    try {
      boost::system::error_code ec;
      iosvc->run(ec);
      if(ec) {
        global_stream_lock.lock();
        std::cout << "Message: " << ec << ".\n";
        global_stream_lock.unlock();
      }
      break;
    }
    catch(std::exception &ex) {
      global_stream_lock.lock();
```

```
        std::cout << "Message: " << ex.what() << ".\n";
        global_stream_lock.unlock();
      }
    }

    global_stream_lock.lock();
    std::cout << "Thread " << counter << " End.\n";
    global_stream_lock.unlock();
}

void TimerHandler(
  const boost::system::error_code &ec,
  boost::shared_ptr<boost::asio::deadline_timer> tmr,
  boost::shared_ptr<boost::asio::io_service::strand> strand
)
{
  if(ec) {
    global_stream_lock.lock();
    std::cout << "Error Message: " << ec << ".\n";
    global_stream_lock.unlock();
  }
  else {
    global_stream_lock.lock();
    std::cout << "You see this every three seconds.\n";
    global_stream_lock.unlock();

    tmr->expires_from_now( boost::posix_time::seconds(1));
    tmr->async_wait(
      strand->wrap(boost::bind(&TimerHandler, _1, tmr, strand))
    );
  }
}

void Print(int number) {
  std::cout << "Number: " << number << std::endl;
  boost::this_thread::sleep(
  boost::posix_time::milliseconds(500));
}

int main(void) {
  boost::shared_ptr<boost::asio::io_service> io_svc(
    new boost::asio::io_service
  );
```

```
boost::shared_ptr<boost::asio::io_service::work> worker(
  new boost::asio::io_service::work(*io_svc)
);
boost::shared_ptr<boost::asio::io_service::strand> strand(
  new boost::asio::io_service::strand(*io_svc)
);

global_stream_lock.lock();
std::cout << "Press ENTER to exit!\n";
global_stream_lock.unlock();

boost::thread_group threads;
for(int i=1; i<=5; i++)
  threads.create_thread(boost::bind(&WorkerThread, io_svc, i));

boost::this_thread::sleep(boost::posix_time::seconds(1));

strand->post(boost::bind(&Print, 1));
strand->post(boost::bind(&Print, 2));
strand->post(boost::bind(&Print, 3));
strand->post(boost::bind(&Print, 4));
strand->post(boost::bind(&Print, 5));

boost::shared_ptr<boost::asio::deadline_timer> timer(
  new boost::asio::deadline_timer(*io_svc)
);

timer->expires_from_now( boost::posix_time::seconds(1));
timer->async_wait(
  strand->wrap(boost::bind(&TimerHandler, _1, timer, strand))
);

std::cin.get();

io_svc->stop();

threads.join_all();

return 0;
}
```

Save the preceding code as `timer3.cpp` and compile it by running the following command:

```
g++ -Wall -ansi -I ../boost_1_58_0 timer3.cpp -o timer3 -L
../boost_1_58_0/stage/lib -l boost_system-mgw49-mt-1_58 -l ws2_32 -l
libboost_thread-mgw49-mt-1_58
```

Now, run the program by typing the `timer3` command in the console and we will get the following output:

From the output, we can see that the first five `work` objects are executed first because they have to be serially executed and afterwards, the `TimerHandler()` functions are executed. The `work` objects have to be completed first before the timer thread is executed. If we remove the `strand` wrap, the flow of the program will be messy because we do not lock the `std::cout` function inside the `Print()` function.

Summary

We have successfully serialized the `io_service` object's work by using the `strand` object, so we can ensure the order of work we have designed. We can also ensure our program will run smoothly without any crashes by using error and exception handling. Lastly, in this chapter, we discussed the waiting time, since this is important when creating a network application.

Now, let us move on to the next chapter to talk about creating a server-client application that will make communication possible between two parties, the server and the client.

6
Creating a Client-server Application

In the previous chapter, we delved into the `Boost.Asio` libraries, which are important in order to develop a network application. And now, we will move to a deeper discussion about a **client-server** application that can communicate with each other over a computer network between two or more computers. One of them is called **client** and the other one is the **server**.

We are going to discuss the development of the server, which is able to send and receive data traffic from the client and also create a client-side program to receive data traffic. In this chapter, we will discuss the following topics:

- Establishing a connection between the client and server
- Sending and receiving data between the client and server
- Wrapping the most frequently used code to simplify the programming process by avoiding code reuse

Establishing a connection

We talked about two types of Internet Protocol (IP) in *Chapter 2, Understanding the Networking Concepts*. These are Transmission Control Protocol (TCP) and User Datagram Protocol (UDP). TCP is connection-oriented, which means data can be sent just after the connection has been established. In contrast, UDP is connectionless Internet protocol, which means the protocol just sends the data directly to the destination device. In this chapter, we will only talk about TCP; therefore, we have to establish the connection first. Connection can only be established if the two parties, in this case, the client and server, accept the connection. Here, we will try to establish a connection synchronously and asynchronously.

A synchronous client

We start with establishing the synchronous connection to a remote host. It is acting as a client, which will open a connection to the Packt Publishing website (www. packtpub.com). We will use TCP protocol, as we discussed earlier in *Chapter 2, Understanding the Networking Concepts*. Here is the code:

```cpp
/* connectsync.cpp */
#include <boost/asio.hpp>
#include <boost/shared_ptr.hpp>
#include <boost/thread.hpp>
#include <boost/thread/mutex.hpp>
#include <boost/bind.hpp>
#include <boost/lexical_cast.hpp>

boost::mutex global_stream_lock;

void WorkerThread(boost::shared_ptr<boost::asio::io_service>
iosvc, int counter) {
  global_stream_lock.lock();
  std::cout << "Thread " << counter << " Start.\n";
  global_stream_lock.unlock();

  while(true) {
    try {
      boost::system::error_code ec;
      iosvc->run(ec);
      if(ec) {
        global_stream_lock.lock();
        std::cout << "Message: " << ec << ".\n";
        global_stream_lock.unlock();
      }
      break;
    }
    catch(std::exception &ex) {
      global_stream_lock.lock();
      std::cout << "Message: " << ex.what() << ".\n";
      global_stream_lock.unlock();
    }
  }

  global_stream_lock.lock();
  std::cout << "Thread " << counter << " End.\n";
```

```
    global_stream_lock.unlock();
}

int main(void) {
  boost::shared_ptr<boost::asio::io_service> io_svc(
    new boost::asio::io_service
  );

  boost::shared_ptr<boost::asio::io_service::work> worker(
    new boost::asio::io_service::work(*io_svc)
  );
  boost::shared_ptr<boost::asio::io_service::strand> strand(
    new boost::asio::io_service::strand(*io_svc)
  );

  global_stream_lock.lock();
  std::cout << "Press ENTER to exit!\n";
  global_stream_lock.unlock();

  boost::thread_group threads;
  for(int i=1; i<=2; i++)
    threads.create_thread(boost::bind(&WorkerThread, io_svc, i));

  boost::asio::ip::tcp::socket sckt(*io_svc);

  try {
    boost::asio::ip::tcp::resolver resolver(*io_svc);
    boost::asio::ip::tcp::resolver::query
    query("www.packtpub.com",
      boost::lexical_cast<std::string>(80)
    );
    boost::asio::ip::tcp::resolver::iterator iterator =
    resolver.resolve(query);
    boost::asio::ip::tcp::endpoint endpoint = *iterator;

    global_stream_lock.lock();
    std::cout << "Connecting to: " << endpoint << std::endl;
    global_stream_lock.unlock();

    sckt.connect(endpoint);
    std::cout << "Connected!\n";
  }
  catch(std::exception &ex) {
    global_stream_lock.lock();
```

```
        std::cout << "Message: " << ex.what() << ".\n";
        global_stream_lock.unlock();
    }

    std::cin.get();

    boost::system::error_code ec;
    sckt.shutdown(boost::asio::ip::tcp::socket::shutdown_both, ec);
    sckt.close(ec);

    io_svc->stop();

    threads.join_all();

    return 0;
}
```

Save the preceding code as connectsync.cpp and run the following command to compile the code:

```
g++ -Wall -ansi -I ../boost_1_58_0 connectsync.cpp -o connectsync -L
../boost_1_58_0/stage/lib -l boost_system-mgw49-mt-1_58 -l ws2_32 -l
libboost_thread-mgw49-mt-1_58
```

Run the program by typing connectsync in the console, and we should get the following output:

```
C:\Windows\system32\cmd.exe                                          _  □  ✕

C:\CPP>g++ -Wall -ansi -I ../boost_1_58_0 connectsync.cpp -o connectsync -L ../b
oost_1_58_0/stage/lib -l boost_system-mgw49-mt-1_58 -l ws2_32 -l libboost_thread
-mgw49-mt-1_58

C:\CPP>connectsync
Press ENTER to exit!
Thread 2 Start.
Thread 1 Start.
Connecting to: 83.166.169.231:80

Thread 1 End.
Thread 2 End.

C:\CPP>
```

The program will exit as soon as we press the *Enter* key.

Now, let us analyze the code. As we can see in the preceding code, we use our previous sample code and insert a line of code in order to make it able to establish a connection. Let's draw our attention to the line we have inserted:

```
boost::asio::ip::tcp::socket sckt(*io_svc);
```

We now have a global variable, which is `socket`. This variable will be used to provide socket functionality. It comes from the namespace `boost::asio::ip::tcp` because we use TCP as our protocol:

```
boost::asio::ip::tcp::resolver resolver(*io_svc);
boost::asio::ip::tcp::resolver::query query("www.packtpub.com",
  boost::lexical_cast<std::string>(80)
);
boost::asio::ip::tcp::resolver::iterator iterator =
resolver.resolve(query);
```

We also use the namespace `boost::asio::ip::tcp::resolver`. It is used to get the address of the remote host we that want to connect with. With the `query()` class, we pass the Internet address and port as a parameter. But because we use an integer type for a port number, we have to convert it to a string by using `lexical_cast`. The query class is used to describe the query that can be passed to a resolver. Then, by using the `iterator` class, we will define iterators from the results returned by a resolver:

```
boost::asio::ip::tcp::endpoint endpoint = *iterator;
```

After the iterator is successfully created, we give it to the `endpoint` type variable. The endpoint will store the list of `ip` addresses that are generated by the `resolver`:

```
sckt.connect(endpoint);
```

Then, the `connect()` member function will connect the socket to the endpoint, which we specified before. If everything runs properly and no error or exception is thrown, the connection is now established:

```
boost::system::error_code ec;
sckt.shutdown(boost::asio::ip::tcp::socket::shutdown_both, ec);
sckt.close(ec);
```

To release the connection, we have to disable the sending and receiving data process on the socket first by using the `shutdown()` member function; then, we invoke the `close()` member function to close the socket.

When we run the program and get output like the preceding image, it will inform us that the connection has been established. We can change the port number, for example, to `110`, which is Remote TELNET Service protocol, in the `query()` class like the following:

```
boost::asio::ip::tcp::resolver::query query("www.packtpub.com",
  boost::lexical_cast<std::string>(110)
);
```

Then, the program will throw an exception, and the output will be as follows:

From the output, we can conclude that the connection has been refused by the target machine because the port we plan to connect to is closed. This means that by using port 80, which is **Hypertext Transfer Protocol (HTTP)**, we can make a connection with the Packt Publishing website.

An asynchronous client

We have already been able to establish a connection synchronously. But how about if we need to connect asynchronously to the target so that the program will not freeze while trying to make a connection? Let us take a look at the following code to find the answer:

```
/* connectasync.cpp */
#include <boost/asio.hpp>
#include <boost/shared_ptr.hpp>
#include <boost/thread.hpp>
#include <boost/thread/mutex.hpp>
#include <boost/bind.hpp>
#include <boost/lexical_cast.hpp>
#include <iostream>
#include <string>

boost::mutex global_stream_lock;

void WorkerThread(boost::shared_ptr<boost::asio::io_service>
iosvc, int counter) {
  global_stream_lock.lock();
  std::cout << "Thread " << counter << " Start.\n";
  global_stream_lock.unlock();

  while(true) {
    try {
      boost::system::error_code ec;
```

```
      iosvc->run(ec);
      if(ec) {
        global_stream_lock.lock();
        std::cout << "Message: " << ec << ".\n";
        global_stream_lock.unlock();
      }
      break;
    }
    catch(std::exception &ex) {
      global_stream_lock.lock();
      std::cout << "Message: " << ex.what() << ".\n";
      global_stream_lock.unlock();
    }
  }

  global_stream_lock.lock();
  std::cout << "Thread " << counter << " End.\n";
  global_stream_lock.unlock();
}

void OnConnect(const boost::system::error_code &ec) {
  if(ec) {
    global_stream_lock.lock();
    std::cout << "OnConnect Error: " << ec << ".\n";
    global_stream_lock.unlock();
  }
  else {
    global_stream_lock.lock();
    std::cout << "Connected!.\n";
    global_stream_lock.unlock();
  }
}

int main(void) {
  boost::shared_ptr<boost::asio::io_service> io_svc(
    new boost::asio::io_service
  );

  boost::shared_ptr<boost::asio::io_service::work> worker(
    new boost::asio::io_service::work(*io_svc)
  );

  boost::shared_ptr<boost::asio::io_service::strand> strand(
    new boost::asio::io_service::strand(*io_svc)
```

```
);

global_stream_lock.lock();
std::cout << "Press ENTER to exit!\n";
global_stream_lock.unlock();

boost::thread_group threads;
for(int i=1; i<=2; i++)
  threads.create_thread(boost::bind(&WorkerThread, io_svc, i));

boost::shared_ptr<boost::asio::ip::tcp::socket> sckt(
  new boost::asio::ip::tcp::socket(*io_svc)
);

try {
  boost::asio::ip::tcp::resolver resolver(*io_svc);
  boost::asio::ip::tcp::resolver::query
  query("www.packtpub.com",
    boost::lexical_cast<std::string>(80)
  );
  boost::asio::ip::tcp::resolver::iterator iterator =
  resolver.resolve( query );
  boost::asio::ip::tcp::endpoint endpoint = *iterator;

  global_stream_lock.lock();
  std::cout << "Connecting to: " << endpoint << std::endl;
  global_stream_lock.unlock();

  sckt->async_connect(endpoint, boost::bind(OnConnect, _1));
}
catch(std::exception &ex) {
  global_stream_lock.lock();
  std::cout << "Message: " << ex.what() << ".\n";
  global_stream_lock.unlock();
}

std::cin.get();

boost::system::error_code ec;
sckt->shutdown(boost::asio::ip::tcp::socket::shutdown_both, ec);
sckt->close(ec);

io_svc->stop();
```

```
    threads.join_all();

    return 0;
}
```

Then, save the preceding code as `connectasync.cpp` and run the following command to compile the code:

```
g++ -Wall -ansi -I ../boost_1_58_0 connectasync.cpp -o connectasync -
L ../boost_1_58_0/stage/lib -l boost_system-mgw49-mt-1_58 -l ws2_32 -
l libboost_thread-mgw49-mt-1_58
```

Try to run the program, and you should get the following output:

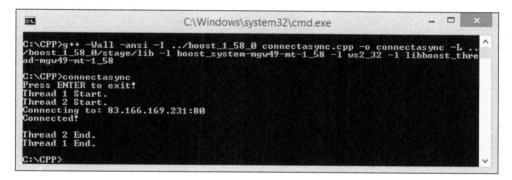

As we can see in the preceding code, we add the `OnConnect()` function. Because the `socket` object is noncopyable, and we need to ensure that it is still valid while the handler is waiting to be called, we have to use the `boost::shared_ptr` namespace. We also use the `boost::bind` namespace to invoke the handler, that is, the `OnConnect()` function.

An asynchronous server

We already know how to connect to a remote host synchronously and asynchronously. Now, we are going to create the server program to talk with the client-side program that we created before. Because we will deal with the asynchronous program in the `boost::asio` namespace, we will discuss the client-side program in an asynchronous server only. Let us take a look at the following code:

```
/* serverasync.cpp */
#include <boost/asio.hpp>
#include <boost/shared_ptr.hpp>
#include <boost/thread.hpp>
```

```cpp
#include <boost/thread/mutex.hpp>
#include <boost/bind.hpp>
#include <boost/lexical_cast.hpp>
#include <iostream>
#include <string>

boost::mutex global_stream_lock;

void WorkerThread(boost::shared_ptr<boost::asio::io_service>
iosvc, int counter) {
  global_stream_lock.lock();
  std::cout << "Thread " << counter << " Start.\n";
  global_stream_lock.unlock();

  while(true) {
    try {
      boost::system::error_code ec;
      iosvc->run(ec);
      if(ec) {
        global_stream_lock.lock();
        std::cout << "Message: " << ec << ".\n";
        global_stream_lock.unlock();
      }
      break;
    }
    catch(std::exception &ex) {
      global_stream_lock.lock();
      std::cout << "Message: " << ex.what() << ".\n";
      global_stream_lock.unlock();
    }
  }

  global_stream_lock.lock();
  std::cout << "Thread " << counter << " End.\n";
  global_stream_lock.unlock();
}

void OnAccept(const boost::system::error_code &ec) {
  if(ec) {
    global_stream_lock.lock();
    std::cout << "OnAccept Error: " << ec << ".\n";
    global_stream_lock.unlock();
  }
  else {
```

```
      global_stream_lock.lock();
      std::cout << "Accepted!" << ".\n";
      global_stream_lock.unlock();
  }
}

int main(void) {
  boost::shared_ptr<boost::asio::io_service> io_svc(
    new boost::asio::io_service
  );

  boost::shared_ptr<boost::asio::io_service::work> worker(
    new boost::asio::io_service::work(*io_svc)
  );

  boost::shared_ptr<boost::asio::io_service::strand> strand(
    new boost::asio::io_service::strand(*io_svc)
  );

  global_stream_lock.lock();
  std::cout << "Press ENTER to exit!\n";
  global_stream_lock.unlock();

  boost::thread_group threads;
  for(int i=1; i<=2; i++)
    threads.create_thread(boost::bind(&WorkerThread, io_svc, i));

  boost::shared_ptr< boost::asio::ip::tcp::acceptor > acceptor(
    new boost::asio::ip::tcp::acceptor(*io_svc)
  );

  boost::shared_ptr<boost::asio::ip::tcp::socket> sckt(
    new boost::asio::ip::tcp::socket(*io_svc)
  );

  try {
    boost::asio::ip::tcp::resolver resolver(*io_svc);
    boost::asio::ip::tcp::resolver::query query(
      "127.0.0.1",
      boost::lexical_cast<std::string>(4444)
    );
    boost::asio::ip::tcp::endpoint endpoint =
    *resolver.resolve(query);
    acceptor->open(endpoint.protocol());
```

```
        acceptor->set_option(
          boost::asio::ip::tcp::acceptor::reuse_address(false));
        acceptor->bind(endpoint);
        acceptor->listen(boost::asio::socket_base::max_connections);
        acceptor->async_accept(*sckt, boost::bind(OnAccept, _1));

        global_stream_lock.lock();
        std::cout << "Listening on: " << endpoint << std::endl;
        global_stream_lock.unlock();
    }
    catch(std::exception &ex) {
        global_stream_lock.lock();
        std::cout << "Message: " << ex.what() << ".\n";
        global_stream_lock.unlock();
    }

    std::cin.get();

    boost::system::error_code ec;
    acceptor->close(ec);

    sckt->shutdown(boost::asio::ip::tcp::socket::shutdown_both, ec);
    sckt->close(ec);

    io_svc->stop();

    threads.join_all();

    return 0;
}
```

Save the preceding code as `serverasync.cpp` and run the following command to compile the code:

```
g++ -Wall -ansi -I ../boost_1_58_0 serverasync.cpp -o serverasync -L
../boost_1_58_0/stage/lib -l boost_system-mgw49-mt-1_58 -l ws2_32 -l
libboost_thread-mgw49-mt-1_58 -l mswsock
```

Before we run the program, let us distinguish the code. We now have a new object, which is `tcp::acceptor`. This object is used for accepting new socket connections. Due to the use of the `accept()` function, we need to add the `mswsock` library to our compilation process:

```
    acptor->open(endpoint.protocol());
    acptor->set_option
```

```
(boost::asio::ip::tcp::acceptor::reuse_address(false));
acptor->bind(endpoint);
acptor->listen(boost::asio::socket_base::max_connections);
acptor->async_accept(*sckt, boost::bind(OnAccept, _1));
```

From the preceding code snippet, we can see that the program calls the `open()` function to open the acceptor by using the protocol that is retrieved from the `endpoint` variable. Then, by using the `set_option` function, we set an option on the acceptor to not reuse the address. The acceptor is also bound to the endpoint using the `bind()` function. After that, we invoke the `listen()` function to put the acceptor into the state where it will listen for new connections. Finally, the acceptor will accept new connections by using the `async_accept()` function, which will start an asynchronous accept.

Now, it is time to run the program. We need to open two command consoles here. The first console is for the program itself and the second is for calling `telnet` command to make a connection to the server. We only need to run the command `telnet 127.0.0.1 4444` just after we run the `serverasync` program (we can refer to *Chapter 2, Understanding the Networking Concepts,* to call the `telnet` command in the command prompt). The output should be like the following:

From the preceding image, we can see that the program is listening to port `4444` when it starts, and after we call the `telnet` command to start a connection to port `4444`, the program accepts the connection. However, because we only have one socket object and invoke the `async_accept()` function just once, the program will accept one connection only.

Reading and writing to the socket

We are officially able to make a client-server connection. Now, we are going to write and read the socket to make the connection more useful. We will modify our previous code, serverasync.cpp, and add the basic_stream_socket object, which provides stream-oriented socket functionality.

 To get more detailed information about the basic_stream_socket object, you can visit www.boost.org/doc/libs/1_58_0/doc/html/boost_asio/reference/basic_stream_socket.html.

Now, take a look at the following code containing the read and write socket process:

```cpp
/* readwritesocket.cpp */
#include <boost/asio.hpp>
#include <boost/shared_ptr.hpp>
#include <boost/thread.hpp>
#include <boost/thread/mutex.hpp>
#include <boost/bind.hpp>
#include <boost/lexical_cast.hpp>
#include <boost/cstdint.hpp>
#include <boost/enable_shared_from_this.hpp>
#include <iostream>
#include <string>

boost::mutex global_stream_lock;

void WorkerThread(boost::shared_ptr<boost::asio::io_service>
iosvc, int counter) {
  global_stream_lock.lock();
  std::cout << "Thread " << counter << " Start.\n";
  global_stream_lock.unlock();

  while(true) {
    try {
      boost::system::error_code ec;
      iosvc->run(ec);
      if(ec) {
        global_stream_lock.lock();
        std::cout << "Message: " << ec << ".\n";
        global_stream_lock.unlock();
      }
```

```
      break;
    }
    catch(std::exception &ex) {
      global_stream_lock.lock();
      std::cout << "Message: " << ex.what() << ".\n";
      global_stream_lock.unlock();
    }
  }

  global_stream_lock.lock();
  std::cout << "Thread " << counter << " End.\n";
  global_stream_lock.unlock();
}

struct ClientContext : public
boost::enable_shared_from_this<ClientContext> {
  boost::asio::ip::tcp::socket m_socket;

  std::vector<boost::uint8_t> m_recv_buffer;
  size_t m_recv_buffer_index;

  std::list<std::vector<boost::uint8_t> > m_send_buffer;

  ClientContext(boost::asio::io_service & io_service)
  : m_socket(io_service), m_recv_buffer_index(0) {
    m_recv_buffer.resize(4096);
  }

  ~ClientContext() {
  }

  void Close() {
    boost::system::error_code ec;
    m_socket.shutdown(boost::asio::ip::tcp::socket::shutdown_both,
    ec);
    m_socket.close(ec);
  }

  void OnSend(const boost::system::error_code &ec,
  std::list<std::vector<boost::uint8_t> >::iterator itr) {
    if(ec) {
      global_stream_lock.lock();
      std::cout << "OnSend Error: " << ec << ".\n";
```

```
        global_stream_lock.unlock();

        Close();
    }
    else {
      global_stream_lock.lock();
      std::cout << "Sent " << (*itr).size() << " bytes." <<
      std::endl;
      global_stream_lock.unlock();
    }
    m_send_buffer.erase(itr);

    // Start the next pending send
    if(!m_send_buffer.empty()) {
      boost::asio::async_write(
        m_socket,
        boost::asio::buffer(m_send_buffer.front()),
        boost::bind(
          &ClientContext::OnSend,
          shared_from_this(),
          boost::asio::placeholders::error,
          m_send_buffer.begin()
        )
      );
    }
  }

  void Send(const void * buffer, size_t length) {
    bool can_send_now = false;

    std::vector<boost::uint8_t> output;
    std::copy((const boost::uint8_t *)buffer, (const
    boost::uint8_t *)buffer + length, std::back_inserter(output));

    // Store if this is the only current send or not
    can_send_now = m_send_buffer.empty();

    // Save the buffer to be sent
    m_send_buffer.push_back(output);

    // Only send if there are no more pending buffers waiting!
    if(can_send_now) {
      // Start the next pending send
      boost::asio::async_write(
```

```
            m_socket,
            boost::asio::buffer(m_send_buffer.front()),
            boost::bind(
               &ClientContext::OnSend,
               shared_from_this(),
               boost::asio::placeholders::error,
               m_send_buffer.begin()
            )
         );
      }
   }


   void OnRecv(const boost::system::error_code &ec, size_t
   bytes_transferred) {
      if(ec) {
         global_stream_lock.lock();
         std::cout << "OnRecv Error: " << ec << ".\n";
         global_stream_lock.unlock();

         Close();
      }
      else {
         // Increase how many bytes we have saved up
         m_recv_buffer_index += bytes_transferred;

         // Debug information
         global_stream_lock.lock();
         std::cout << "Recv " << bytes_transferred << " bytes." <<
         std::endl;
         global_stream_lock.unlock();

         // Dump all the data
         global_stream_lock.lock();
         for(size_t x = 0; x < m_recv_buffer_index; ++x) {

            std::cout << (char)m_recv_buffer[x] << " ";
            if((x + 1) % 16 == 0) {
               std::cout << std::endl;
            }
         }
         std::cout << std::endl << std::dec;
         global_stream_lock.unlock();
```

```
        // Clear all the data
        m_recv_buffer_index = 0;

        // Start the next receive cycle
        Recv();
      }
    }

    void Recv() {
      m_socket.async_read_some(
        boost::asio::buffer(
          &m_recv_buffer[m_recv_buffer_index],
          m_recv_buffer.size() - m_recv_buffer_index),
        boost::bind(&ClientContext::OnRecv, shared_from_this(), _1,
        _2)
      );
    }
};

void OnAccept(const boost::system::error_code &ec,
boost::shared_ptr<ClientContext> clnt) {
  if(ec) {
    global_stream_lock.lock();
    std::cout << "OnAccept Error: " << ec << ".\n";
    global_stream_lock.unlock();
  }
  else {
    global_stream_lock.lock();
    std::cout << "Accepted!" << ".\n";
    global_stream_lock.unlock();

    // 2 bytes message size, followed by the message
    clnt->Send("Hi there!", 9);
    clnt->Recv();
  }
}

int main(void) {
  boost::shared_ptr<boost::asio::io_service> io_svc(
    new boost::asio::io_service
  );

  boost::shared_ptr<boost::asio::io_service::work> worker(
    new boost::asio::io_service::work(*io_svc)
```

```
  );

  boost::shared_ptr<boost::asio::io_service::strand> strand(
    new boost::asio::io_service::strand(*io_svc)
  );

  global_stream_lock.lock();
  std::cout << "Press ENTER to exit!\n";
  global_stream_lock.unlock();

  // We just use one worker thread
  // in order that no thread safety issues
  boost::thread_group threads;
  threads.create_thread(boost::bind(&WorkerThread, io_svc, 1));

  boost::shared_ptr< boost::asio::ip::tcp::acceptor > acceptor(
    new boost::asio::ip::tcp::acceptor(*io_svc)
  );

  boost::shared_ptr<ClientContext> client(
    new ClientContext(*io_svc)
  );

  try {
    boost::asio::ip::tcp::resolver resolver(*io_svc);
    boost::asio::ip::tcp::resolver::query query(
      "127.0.0.1",
      boost::lexical_cast<std::string>(4444)
    );
    boost::asio::ip::tcp::endpoint endpoint =
    *resolver.resolve(query);
    acceptor->open(endpoint.protocol());
    acceptor->set_option(boost::asio::ip::tcp::acceptor::
    reuse_address(false));
    acceptor->bind(endpoint);
    acceptor->listen(boost::asio::socket_base::max_connections);
    acceptor->async_accept(client->m_socket, boost::bind(OnAccept,
    _1, client));

    global_stream_lock.lock();
    std::cout << "Listening on: " << endpoint << std::endl;
    global_stream_lock.unlock();
  }
```

```
catch(std::exception &ex) {
  global_stream_lock.lock();
  std::cout << "Message: " << ex.what() << ".\n";
  global_stream_lock.unlock();
}

std::cin.get();

boost::system::error_code ec;
acceptor->close(ec);

io_svc->stop();

threads.join_all();

return 0;
}
```

Save the preceding code as `readwritesocket.cpp` and compile the code using the following command:

```
g++ -Wall -ansi -I ../boost_1_58_0 readwritesocket.cpp -o
readwritesocket -L ../boost_1_58_0/stage/lib -l boost_system-mgw49-
mt-1_58 -l ws2_32 -l libboost_thread-mgw49-mt-1_58 -l mswsock
```

If we compare the code of the `readwritesocket.cpp` file with the `serverasync.cpp` file, we will find that we add a new class called `ClientContext`. It contains five member functions: `Send()`, `OnSend()`, `Recv()`, `OnRecv()`, and `Close()`.

The Send() and OnSend() functions

In the `Send()` function, we input an array of characters and their length. Before the function sends the array of characters, it has to check whether or not the `m_send_buffer` parameter is empty. The sending process can only occur if the buffer is not empty.

The `boost::asio::async_write` namespace writes the socket and invokes the `OnSend()` function handler. Then, it erases the buffer and sends the next pending data if there is any. Now, every time we press any key in the `telnet` window, it will display what we have typed because the `readwritesocket` project sends back what we type to the `telnet` window.

The Recv() and OnRecv() functions

In contrast to the `Send()` function, the `Recv()` function will call the `async_read_some()` function to receive the set of data, and the `OnRecv()` function handler will format the received data to hexadecimal formatting.

Wrapping the network code

For our convenience, let us create a wrapper for a networking application. In using this wrapper, we do not need to reuse our code over and over again; thus, making our programming process simpler and more efficient. For now, just create two files called `wrapper.h` and `wrapper.cpp`, and we will include them in the compilation process in our next code. Because the source codes are quite long in length and will not be convenient to print in this book, I have made them into downloadable files that you can access in this book's repository at `www.packtpub.com/networking-and-servers/boostasio-c-network-programming-second-edition`. Go to the **Code Files** section.

Developing a client and server program

We have already had the network wrapper code simplify our programming process in developing a network application by using the `Boost.Asio` library. Now, let us create a client and server program by using our wrapper code.

Creating a simple echo server

We are going to create a server program that will echo out all traffic it retrieves from the client. In this case, we will use the `telnet` as the client, as we've done previously. The file has to be saved as `echoserver.cpp`, and the content will look like the following:

```
/* echoserver.cpp */
#include "wrapper.h"
#include <conio.h>
#include <boost/thread/mutex.hpp>

boost::mutex global_stream_lock;

class MyConnection : public Connection {
private:
  void OnAccept(const std::string &host, uint16_t port) {
    global_stream_lock.lock();
```

```
        std::cout << "[OnAccept] " << host << ":" << port << "\n";
        global_stream_lock.unlock();

      Recv();
    }

    void OnConnect(const std::string & host, uint16_t port) {
      global_stream_lock.lock();
        std::cout << "[OnConnect] " << host << ":" << port << "\n";
      global_stream_lock.unlock();

      Recv();
    }

    void OnSend(const std::vector<uint8_t> & buffer) {
      global_stream_lock.lock();
        std::cout << "[OnSend] " << buffer.size() << " bytes\n";
        for(size_t x=0; x<buffer.size(); x++) {

          std::cout << (char)buffer[x];
          if((x + 1) % 16 == 0)
            std::cout << std::endl;
        }
        std::cout << std::endl;
        global_stream_lock.unlock();
    }

    void OnRecv(std::vector<uint8_t> &buffer) {
      global_stream_lock.lock();
        std::cout << "[OnRecv] " << buffer.size() << " bytes\n";
        for(size_t x=0; x<buffer.size(); x++) {

          std::cout << (char)buffer[x];
          if((x + 1) % 16 == 0)
            std::cout << std::endl;
        }
        std::cout << std::endl;
        global_stream_lock.unlock();

        // Start the next receive
        Recv();

        // Echo the data back
        Send(buffer);
```

```
    }

    void OnTimer(const boost::posix_time::time_duration &delta) {
      global_stream_lock.lock();
      std::cout << "[OnTimer] " << delta << "\n";
      global_stream_lock.unlock();
    }

    void OnError(const boost::system::error_code &error) {
      global_stream_lock.lock();
      std::cout << "[OnError] " << error << "\n";
      global_stream_lock.unlock();
    }

public:
  MyConnection(boost::shared_ptr<Hive> hive)
    : Connection(hive) {
  }

  ~MyConnection() {
  }
};

class MyAcceptor : public Acceptor {
private:
  bool OnAccept(boost::shared_ptr<Connection> connection, const
  std::string &host, uint16_t port) {
    global_stream_lock.lock();
    std::cout << "[OnAccept] " << host << ":" << port << "\n";
    global_stream_lock.unlock();

    return true;
  }

  void OnTimer(const boost::posix_time::time_duration &delta) {
    global_stream_lock.lock();
    std::cout << "[OnTimer] " << delta << "\n";
    global_stream_lock.unlock();
  }

  void OnError(const boost::system::error_code &error) {
    global_stream_lock.lock();
    std::cout << "[OnError] " << error << "\n";
    global_stream_lock.unlock();
```

```
      }

  public:
    MyAcceptor(boost::shared_ptr<Hive> hive)
      : Acceptor(hive) {
    }

    ~MyAcceptor() {
    }
};

int main(void) {
  boost::shared_ptr<Hive> hive(new Hive());

  boost::shared_ptr<MyAcceptor> acceptor(new MyAcceptor(hive));
  acceptor->Listen("127.0.0.1", 4444);

  boost::shared_ptr<MyConnection> connection(new
  MyConnection(hive));
  acceptor->Accept(connection);

  while(!_kbhit()) {
    hive->Poll();
    Sleep(1);
  }

  hive->Stop();

  return 0;
}
```

Then, compile the preceding code using the following command. Here, we can see that we include wrapper.cpp in the compilation process to take advantage of our wrapper code:

```
g++ -Wall -ansi -I ../boost_1_58_0 wrapper.cpp echoserver.cpp -o
echoserver -L ../boost_1_58_0/stage/lib -l boost_system-mgw49-mt-1_58
-l ws2_32 -l libboost_thread-mgw49-mt-1_58 -l mswsock
```

We can try the preceding program by typing `echoserver` in the console window; after which, we should get output like the following:

```
C:\CPP>echoserver
[OnTimer] 00:00:01.007680
[OnTimer] 00:00:01.009309
[OnTimer] 00:00:01.000313
[OnTimer] 00:00:01.014195
[OnTimer] 00:00:01.001534
[OnTimer] 00:00:01.000240
[OnTimer] 00:00:01.007600
[OnTimer] 00:00:01.007444
[OnTimer] 00:00:01.001393
[OnTimer] 00:00:01.007431
[OnTimer] 00:00:01.014495
[OnTimer] 00:00:01.001507
```

The first time we run the program, it will listen to port 4444 in localhost. We can see in the main block that the program calls the poll() function in the Hive class if there is no keyboard hit. This means that the program will close if any key is pressed because it will invoke the Stop() function in the Hive class, which will stop the io_service object. Every 1000 milliseconds, the timer will tick because the constructor of the Acceptor class initiates the interval of the timer for 1000 milliseconds.

Now, open another console window and type the command telnet 127.0.0.1 4444 to make telnet our client. After the echoserver accepts the connection, every time we press the alphanumeric option on the keyboard, the echoserver will send the character back to telnet. The following image describes the acceptance connection between the echoserver and the telnet server:

```
[OnAccept] 127.0.0.1:57507
[OnAccept] 127.0.0.1:4444
[OnTimer] 00:00:01.001923
[OnRecv] 1 bytes
A
[OnSend] 1 bytes
A
[OnTimer] 00:00:01.000316
[OnRecv] 1 bytes
B
[OnSend] 1 bytes
B
[OnTimer] 00:00:01.001034
[OnTimer] 00:00:01.000442
[OnRecv] 1 bytes
C
[OnSend] 1 bytes
C
[OnTimer] 00:00:01.001932
[OnTimer] 00:00:01.000447
```

When the server accepts the connection from the client, the `OnAccept()` function handler will be invoked immediately. I pressed the *A*, *B*, and *C* keys respectively in the `telnet` window, and then `echoserver` received the characters and sent them back to the client. The `telnet` window also displays A, B, and C.

Creating a simple client program

We have successfully created a server-side program. Now, we will move on to develop the client-side program. It will receive the content of the Packt Publishing website through the `HTTP GET` command, and the code will be like the following:

```cpp
/* clienthttpget.cpp */
#include "wrapper.h"
#include <conio.h>
#include <boost/thread/mutex.hpp>

boost::mutex global_stream_lock;

class MyConnection : public Connection {
private:
  void OnAccept(const std::string &host, uint16_t port) {
    global_stream_lock.lock();
    std::cout << "[OnAccept] " << host << ":" << port << "\n";
    global_stream_lock.unlock();

    // Start the next receive
    Recv();
  }

  void OnConnect(const std::string &host, uint16_t port) {
    global_stream_lock.lock();
    std::cout << "[OnConnect] " << host << ":" << port << "\n";
    global_stream_lock.unlock();

    // Start the next receive
    Recv();

    std::string str = "GET / HTTP/1.0\r\n\r\n";

    std::vector<uint8_t> request;
    std::copy(str.begin(), str.end(),
    std::back_inserter(request));
```

```
      Send(request);
  }

  void OnSend(const std::vector<uint8_t> &buffer) {
    global_stream_lock.lock();
    std::cout << "[OnSend] " << buffer.size() << " bytes\n";
    for(size_t x=0; x<buffer.size(); x++) {

      std::cout << (char)buffer[x];
      if((x + 1) % 16 == 0)
        std::cout << "\n";
    }
    std::cout << "\n";
    global_stream_lock.unlock();
  }

  void OnRecv(std::vector<uint8_t> &buffer) {
    global_stream_lock.lock();
    std::cout << "[OnRecv] " << buffer.size() << " bytes\n";
    for(size_t x=0; x<buffer.size(); x++) {

      std::cout << (char)buffer[x];
      if((x + 1) % 16 == 0)
        std::cout << "\n";
    }
    std::cout << "\n";
    global_stream_lock.unlock();

    // Start the next receive
    Recv();
  }

  void OnTimer(const boost::posix_time::time_duration &delta) {
    global_stream_lock.lock();
    std::cout << "[OnTimer] " << delta << std::endl;
    global_stream_lock.unlock();
  }

  void OnError(const boost::system::error_code &error) {
    global_stream_lock.lock();
    std::cout << "[OnError] " << error << "\n";
    global_stream_lock.unlock();
  }
```

```
public:
  MyConnection(boost::shared_ptr<Hive> hive)
    : Connection(hive) {
  }

  ~MyConnection() {
  }
};

int main(void) {
  boost::shared_ptr<Hive> hive(new Hive());

  boost::shared_ptr<MyConnection> connection(new
  MyConnection(hive));
  connection->Connect("www.packtpub.com", 80);

  while(!_kbhit()) {
    hive->Poll();
    Sleep(1);
  }

  hive->Stop();

  return 0;
}
```

Save the preceding code as `clienthttpget.cpp`, and compile the code using the following command:

```
g++ -Wall -ansi -I ../boost_1_58_0 wrapper.cpp clienthttpget.cpp -o
clienthttpget -L ../boost_1_58_0/stage/lib -l boost_system-mgw49-mt-
1_58 -l ws2_32 -l libboost_thread-mgw49-mt-1_58 -l mswsock
```

When we run the program, the following output will be displayed:

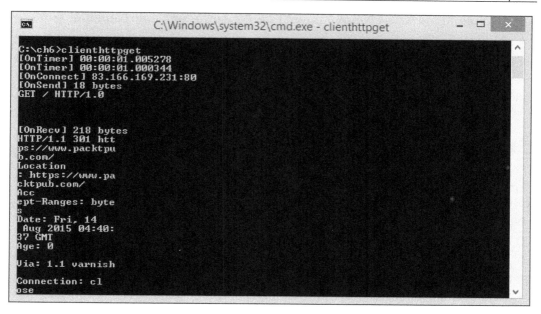

Just after the connection is established, the program sends an HTTP GET command to port 80 of www.packtpub.com using the following code snippet:

```
std::string str = "GET / HTTP/1.0\r\n\r\n";
std::vector<uint8_t> request;
std::copy(str.begin(), str.end(), std::back_inserter(request));
Send(request)
```

It then sends the request to the socket using the Send() function in the Connection class inside the code of the wrapper.cpp file. The code snippet of the Send() function is as follows:

```
m_io_strand.post(boost::bind(&Connection::DispatchSend,
shared_from_this(), buffer));
```

As we can see, we use the strand object in order to allow all events to be serially run. In addition, because of the strand object, we do not have to use the lock object every time the event occurs.

After the request is sent, the program will pool the incoming data using the following code snippet:

```
m_io_service.poll();
```

Then, once the data is coming, it will be displayed in the console by the OnRecv() function handler, as we can see in the preceding image.

Summary

There are three basic steps when it comes to developing a network application. The first step includes establishing a connection between the source and target, which means the client and server. We can configure the socket object along with the acceptor object to establish the connection.

Secondly, we exchange data by reading and writing to the socket. For this purpose, we can use the basic_stream_socket functions collection. In our previous example, we used the boost::asio::async_write() method to send the data and the boost::asio::async_read() method to receive the data. Finally, the last step is releasing the connection. By using the shutdown() method in the ip::tcp::socket object, we can disable the sending and receiving of data on the socket. Then, invoking the close() method after the shutdown() function will close the socket and free up the handler. We also have already created a wrapper for all functions, which is most frequently used in network application programming by accessing the Boost.Asio library. This means we can develop a network application simply and efficiently since we do not need to reuse code over and over again.

7
Debugging the Code and Solving the Error

We successfully developed a server-client program in the previous chapter. We also smoothly ran the program that we created. However, sometimes, we will face some problems when we run the application, such as receiving an unexpected result or the application crashing during runtime. In this situation, the debugging tool has the ability to help us to solve these problems. While discussing the debugging tool, in this chapter, we will cover the following topics:

- Choosing the debugging tool for our use and keeping it simple and lightweight
- Setting up the debugging tool and preparing the executable file to be debugged
- Familiarizing with commands that are used in the debugging tool

Choosing a debugging tool

Many debugging tools around come with the **Integrated Development Environment** (**IDE**) of the programing language. For instance, **Visual Studio** has a debugging tool for C, C++, C#, and Visual Basic. Alternatively, you may have heard about CodeBlock and Bloodshed Dev-C++, which have their own debugging tools as well. However, if you remember what we discussed in *Chapter 1, Simplifying Your Network Programming in C++*, we decided not to use an IDE because its heavy load will not load much resource to our computer. We need a tool that is lightweight to develop our network application.

Our choice of tool is the **GNU Debugger** (**GDB**). GDB is a powerful debugging tool based on a command-line tool; this means that we don't need the complex **Graphic User Interface** (**GUI**). In other words, all we need is a keyboard, not even a mouse, so the system becomes lightweight as well.

There are four main things that GDB can do to help us solve the code problem, which are as follows:

- **Running our code line-by-line**: When GDB runs our program, we can see which line is being executed at the moment
- **Stopping our code on a specific line**: This is useful when we suspect that a certain line has caused an error
- **Examining the suspected line**: When we successfully stop at the suspected line, we can continue to examine it, for example, by checking the value of the variable involved
- **Changing the value of the variable**: If we find the unexpected variable value that has caused an error, we can replace the value at GDB runtime with our expected value to ensure that the change of the value will solve the problem

Installing a debugging tool

Fortunately, you will not need to install anything else if you followed all the steps related to the installation of MinGW-w64 in *Chapter 1, Simplifying Your Network Programming in C++*, because the installer package contains the GDB tool as well. What we need to do now is to run the GDB tool in our command console to check whether it runs properly.

In any active directory of our command prompt, type the following command:

```
gdb
```

We should get the following output in our console window:

```
C:\CPP>gdb
GNU gdb (GDB) 7.8.1
Copyright (C) 2014 Free Software Foundation, Inc.
License GPLv3+: GNU GPL version 3 or later <http://gnu.org/licenses/gpl.
html>
This is free software: you are free to change and redistribute it.
There is NO WARRANTY, to the extent permitted by law.  Type "show copying"
and "show warranty" for details.
```

```
This GDB was configured as "x86_64-w64-mingw32".
Type "show configuration" for configuration details.
For bug reporting instructions, please see:
<http://www.gnu.org/software/gdb/bugs/>.
Find the GDB manual and other documentation resources online at:
<http://www.gnu.org/software/gdb/documentation/>.
For help, type "help".
Type "apropos word" to search for commands related to "word".
(gdb) _
```

As we can see in the preceding output that we got on the console, we have the version 7.8.1 (this is not the latest version as we just obtained it from the MinGW-w64 installer package). In the last line, we also have (gdb) with a blinking cursor next to it; this means that GDB is ready to receive the command. However, for now, the command we need to know is quit (alternatively, we can use q as a shortcut) to exit the GDB. Just type q and press *Enter*, and you will come back to the command prompt.

Preparing a file for debugging

GDB needs at least one executable file to be debugged. For this purpose, we will go back to the previous chapter to borrow the source code from there. Do you remember that we created a game in *Chapter 1, Simplifying Your Network Programming in C++*, where we had to guess the random number that the computer was thinking of? If you remember, we have the source code, that we saved as rangen.cpp in the first chapter, and we have modified it by adding the Boost library, saving it as rangen_boost. cpp in *Chapter 3, Introducing the Boost C++ Libraries*. In the next section, we will use the rangen_boost.cpp source code to demonstrate the use of GDB. Also, for those who have forgotten the source code, I've rewritten it for you here:

```cpp
/* rangen_boost.cpp */
#include <boost/random/mersenne_twister.hpp>
#include <boost/random/uniform_int_distribution.hpp>
#include <iostream>

int main(void) {
  int guessNumber;
  std::cout << "Select number among 0 to 10: ";
  std::cin >> guessNumber;
  if(guessNumber < 0 || guessNumber > 10) {
    return 1;
  }
  boost::random::mt19937 rng;
```

```
boost::random::uniform_int_distribution<> ten(0,10);
int randomNumber = ten(rng);

if(guessNumber == randomNumber) {
  std::cout << "Congratulation, " << guessNumber << " is your
  lucky number.\n";
}
else {
  std::cout << "Sorry, I'm thinking about number " <<
  randomNumber << "\n";
}
return 0;
}
```

We will modify the compiling command in order for it to be used in GDB. We will use the -g option so that the executable file that is created will contain the debugging information and symbols that will be read by GDB. We will produce the rangen_boost_gdb.exe executable file from the rangen_boost.cpp file, which contains the debugging information and symbols using the following command:

g++ -Wall -ansi -I ../boost_1_58_0 rangen_boost.cpp -o rangen_boost_gdb -g

As we can see in the preceding command, we add the -g option in the compiling command in order to record the debugging information and symbols in the executable file. Now, we should have the file named rangen_boost_gdb.exe in our active directory. In the next section, we will debug it using GDB.

We are only able to debug the executable file that is compiled using the -g option. In other words, we will not be able to debug the executable file without having debugging information and symbols. Also, we cannot debug the source code file (*.cpp file) or header file (*.h file).

Running the program under GDB

After preparing the executable file that contains the debugging information and symbols, let's run GDB to read all the symbols from the file and debug it. Run the following command to start the debugging process:

gdb rangen_boost_gdb

Our output will be as follows:

```
C:\CPP>gdb rangen_boost_gdb

GNU gdb (GDB) 7.8.1

Copyright (C) 2014 Free Software Foundation, Inc.

License GPLv3+: GNU GPL version 3 or later <http://gnu.org/licenses/gpl.html>

This is free software: you are free to change and redistribute it.

There is NO WARRANTY, to the extent permitted by law.  Type "show copying"

and "show warranty" for details.

This GDB was configured as "x86_64-w64-mingw32".

Type "show configuration" for configuration details.

For bug reporting instructions, please see:

<http://www.gnu.org/software/gdb/bugs/>.

Find the GDB manual and other documentation resources online at:

<http://www.gnu.org/software/gdb/documentation/>.

For help, type "help".

Type "apropos word" to search for commands related to "word"...

Reading symbols from rangen_boost_gdb...done.

(gdb) _
```

We got the same output as the previous GDB output, except for the last line before (gdb). This line tells us that GDB has successfully read all the debugging symbols and is ready to initiate the debugging process. In this step, we can also specify the arguments, if our program needs any. Since our program does not need to specify any argument, we can ignore it for now.

Starting the debugging process

To start the debugging process, we can call either the run or start command. The former will start our program under GDB, while the latter will behave similarly but will execute the code line-by-line. The difference is that if we have not yet set the breakpoint, the program will run as usual if we call the run command, whereas the debugger will automatically set the breakpoint in the main block of code, stopping the program if it reaches that point, if we start with the start command.

For now, let's use the `start` command for the debugging process. Just type `start` in the GDB prompt, and the console will append the following output:

```
(gdb) start
Temporary breakpoint 1 at 0x401506: file rangen_boost.cpp, line 10.
Starting program: C:\CPP\rangen_boost_gdb.exe
[New Thread 10856.0x213c]

Temporary breakpoint 1, main () at rangen_boost.cpp:10
10                    std::cout << "Select number among 0 to 10: ";
```

The debugging process is started. From the output, we can find that one breakpoint is created automatically inside the `main` block which is in line 10. When there is no breakpoint, the debugger will choose the first statement inside the main block. That is why we get `line 10` as our automatic breakpoint.

The continuing and stepping debugging process

After we successfully start our program under GDB, the next step is to continue and step. We can use one of the following commands to continue and step the debugging process:

- `continue`: This command will resume the execution of the program until our program completes normally. If it finds a breakpoint, the execution will stop at the line where the breakpoint is set.

- `step`: This command will execute just one more step of our program. The *step* might mean either one line of source code or one machine instruction. If it finds the invocation of function, it will come into the function and run one more step inside the function.

- `next`: This command behaves similar to the `step` command, but it only continues to the next line in the current stack frame. In other words, if the `next` command finds the invocation of a function, it will not come into the function.

For now, let's use the `next` command. Type the `next` command in the GDB prompt just after we call the `start` command. We should get the following output:

```
(gdb) next
Select number among 0 to 10: 11          std::cin >> guessNumber;
```

The GDB executes the 10th line and then continues to the 11th line. We will call the `next` command again to continue the debugging process. However, if we just press the *Enter* key, the GDB will execute our previous command. This is why we now just need to press the *Enter* key, which will give us a blinking cursor. Now, we have to input the number that we guessed to be stored in the `guessNumber` variable. I will input the number 4, but you may enter your favorite number. Press the *Enter* key again to continue debugging as many times as needed to exit the program normally. The following output will be appended:

```
(gdb)
4
12                 if(guessNumber < 0 || guessNumber > 10)
(gdb)
17                 boost::random::mt19937 rng;
(gdb)
19                 boost::random::uniform_int_distribution<> ten(0,10);
(gdb)
20                 int randomNumber = ten(rng);
(gdb)
22                 if(guessNumber == randomNumber)
(gdb)
28                     std::cout << "Sorry, I'm thinking about
number " << randomNumber << "\n";
(gdb)
Sorry, I'm thinking about number 8
30                 return 0;
(gdb)
31         }(gdb)
0x00000000004013b5 in __tmainCRTStartup ()
(gdb)
Single stepping until exit from function __tmainCRTStartup, which has
no line number information.
[Inferior 1 (process 11804) exited normally]
```

As we can see in the preceding output, after we enter the number guessed, the program executes the `if` statement to ensure that the number we entered is not out of range. If our guessing number is valid, the program continues to generate a random number. Our guessing number is then compared with a random number generated by our program. The program will give a different output irrespective of the two numbers being same or not. Unfortunately, my guessing number is different than the random number. You might obtain a different output if you are able to guess the number correctly.

Printing the source code

Sometimes, we may want to examine our source file while we run the debugging process. Since the debugging information and symbol are recorded in our program, GDB can print the source code even if it is an executable file. To print the source code, we can type `list` (or the `l` command for the shortcut) in the GDB prompt. By default, GDB will print ten lines at every invocation of the command. However, we can change this setting using the `set listsize` command. Also, to know the number of lines that will be displayed by the `list` command, we can invoke the `show listsize` command. Let's see the following command line output:

```
(gdb) show listsize
Number of source lines gdb will list by default is 10.
(gdb) set listsize 20
(gdb) show listsize
Number of source lines gdb will list by default is 20.
(gdb) _
```

We increase the number of lines to be displayed using the `list` command. Now, every time the `list` command is invoked, the output will display twenty lines of source code.

The following are several forms of the `list` command, which are the most common:

- `list`: This command will show the source code for as many lines as the list size defines. If we call it again, it will display the remaining lines as many as the list size defines.

- `list [linenumber]`: This command will display the lines centered on `linenumber`. The command `list 10` will display line 5 to line 14 since line 10 is at the center.

- `list [functionname]`: This command will display lines centered on the beginning of the `functionname` variable. The command `list main` will display the `int main(void)` function at the center of list.

- `list [first,last]`: This command will display lines from first to last. The command `list 15,16` will display line 15 and line 16 only.

- `list [,last]`: This command will display lines ending with the `last`. The command `list ,5` will display line 1 to line 5.

- `list [first,]`: This command will display all the lines starting with the specified line as the first. The command `list 5,` will display line 5 to the rest of line if the number of the lines is more than the specified line number. Otherwise, it will display as many lines as the list size setting.

- `list +`: This command will display all the lines following the lines last displayed.

- `list -`: This command will display all the lines preceding the lines last displayed.

Setting and deleting the breakpoint

If we suspect that a line makes an error, we can set a breakpoint in that line so that the debugger stops the debugging process at that line. To set a breakpoint, we can call the `break [linenumber]` command. Consider that we want to stop at line 20, which contains the following code:

```
int randomNumber = ten(rng);
```

Here, we will have to call the `break 20` command just after we load our program under GDB to set a breakpoint at line 20. The following output console illustrates this:

```
(gdb) break 20
Breakpoint 1 at 0x401574: file rangen_boost.cpp, line 20.
(gdb) run
Starting program: C:\CPP\rangen_boost_gdb.exe
[New Thread 1428.0x13f4]
Select number among 0 to 10: 2

Breakpoint 1, main () at rangen_boost.cpp:20
20              int randomNumber = ten(rng);
(gdb) next
22              if(guessNumber == randomNumber)
(gdb)
28                      std::cout << "Sorry, I'm thinking about
number " << randomNumber << "\n";
(gdb)
Sorry, I'm thinking about number 8
30              return 0;
(gdb)
31      }(gdb)
0x00000000004013b5 in __tmainCRTStartup ()
(gdb)
Single stepping until exit from function __tmainCRTStartup,
which has no line number information.
[Inferior 1 (process 1428) exited normally]
(gdb)_
```

In the preceding output console, just after our program is loaded under GDB, we call the `break 20` command. The debugger then sets a new breakpoint at line 20. Instead of calling the `start` command as we previously did, we call the `run` command to execute the program and let it stop when it finds a breakpoint. After we enter our guessing number, 2 for example, the debugger stops at line 20, the line at which we expected it to stop. Then, we call the `next` command to continue the debugger and press the *Enter* key several times until the program exits.

If we want to delete a breakpoint, simply use the `delete N` command, in which N is the order in which all the breakpoints are set. If we do not memorize all the locations of the breakpoints that we set, we can call the `info break` command to get a list of all breakpoints. We can also use the `delete` command (without N), which will delete all breakpoints.

Printing a variable value

We were already able to stop at our desired line. We can also discover the value of the variable that we use in our program. We can call the `print [variablename]` command to print the value of any variable. Using the previous breakpoint, we will print the value of the variable `randomNumber`. Just after the debugger hits the breakpoint in line 20, we will call the print `randomNumber` command. Then, we call the `next` command and print the `randomNumber` variable again. Look at the following illustration of the command invocation:

```
(gdb) break 20
Breakpoint 1 at 0x401574: file rangen_boost.cpp, line 20.
(gdb) run
Starting program: C:\CPP\rangen_boost_gdb.exe
[New Thread 5436.0x1b04]
Select number among 0 to 10: 3

Breakpoint 1, main () at rangen_boost.cpp:20
20                  int randomNumber = ten(rng);
(gdb) print randomNumber
$1 = 0
(gdb) next
22                  if(guessNumber == randomNumber)
(gdb) print randomNumber
$2 = 8
(gdb) _
```

As we can see in the preceding output, the following line is where the breakpoint is set:

```
int randomNumber = ten(rng);
```

Before the line is executed, we peek the value of randomNumber variable. The value of the variable is 0. Then, we call the next command to instruct debugger to execute the line. After that, we peek at the value of the variable again, and this time it is 8. Of course, in this experiment, you might get the different value rather than 8.

Modifying a variable value

We will cheat our program by modifying the value of one of the variables. The value of a variable can be reassigned using the set var [variablename]=[newvalue] command. To ensure the type of the variable that we want to modify, we can call the whatis [variablename] command to get the required type of variable.

Now, let's change the value of the randomNumber variable after the program assigns a random number to the variable. We will restart the debugging process, delete all the breakpoints we set already, set a new breakpoint at line 22, and continue the debugging process by typing the continue command until the debugger hits the breakpoint in line 22. On this condition, we can reassign the value of the randomNumber variable to be exactly the same as the value of the guessNumber variable. Now, call the continue command again. After this, we will be congratulated for guessing the correct number.

For more details, let's take a look at the following output console, which will illustrate the preceding step:

```
(gdb) start
The program being debugged has been started already.
Start it from the beginning? (y or n) y

Temporary breakpoint 2 at 0x401506: file rangen_boost.cpp, line 10.
Starting program: C:\CPP\rangen_boost_gdb.exe
[New Thread 6392.0x1030]

Temporary breakpoint 2, main () at rangen_boost.cpp:10
10                std::cout << "Select number among 0 to 10: ";
(gdb) info break
Num     Type           Disp Enb Address            What
1       breakpoint     keep y   0x0000000000401574 in main()
                                                   at rangen_boost.cpp:20
```

```
(gdb) delete 1
(gdb) info break
No breakpoints or watchpoints.
(gdb) break 22
Breakpoint 3 at 0x40158d: file rangen_boost.cpp, line 22.
(gdb) continue
Continuing.
Select number among 0 to 10: 5

Breakpoint 3, main () at rangen_boost.cpp:22
22                    if(guessNumber == randomNumber)
(gdb) whatis randomNumber
type = int
(gdb) print randomNumber
$3 = 8
(gdb) set var randomNumber=5
(gdb) print randomNumber
$4 = 5
(gdb) continue
Continuing.
Congratulation, 5 is your lucky number.
[Inferior 1 (process 6392) exited normally]
(gdb) _
```

As we can see in the preceding output, when we call the start command, the debugger asks us to stop the previous debugging process since it is still running. Just type the *Y* key and press the *Enter* key to answer the query. We can list all the available breakpoints using the info break command and then delete the desired breakpoint based on the order we get from the info break command. We call the continue command to resume the debugging process, and when the debugger hits the breakpoint, we reassign the randomNumber variable with the value of the guessNumber variable. We continue the debugging process and successfully modify the value of the randomNumber variable at runtime since we are congratulated by the program.

If we have many variables in the program, instead of printing all of the variables one-by-one, we can print the values of all the variables using the info locals command.

Calling the command prompt

I occasionally call the Windows shell command inside the GDB prompt, such as the `cls` command to clear the screen, the `dir` command to list the content of the active directory, and even the compiling command. If you also want to execute the Windows shell command, the GDB command that you can use is `shell [Windows shell command]`. It actually just adds the `shell` command before the Windows shell command and argument when needed. Let's see the following console output to understand executing the Windows shell command inside the GDB prompt. Let's take a look at the following output:

```
C:\CPP>gdb

GNU gdb (GDB) 7.8.1

Copyright (C) 2014 Free Software Foundation, Inc.

License GPLv3+: GNU GPL version 3 or later
<http://gnu.org/licenses/gpl.html>

This is free software: you are free to change and redistribute it.

There is NO WARRANTY, to the extent permitted by law.  Type "show
copying"

and "show warranty" for details.

This GDB was configured as "x86_64-w64-mingw32".

Type "show configuration" for configuration details.

For bug reporting instructions, please see:

<http://www.gnu.org/software/gdb/bugs/>.

Find the GDB manual and other documentation resources online at:

<http://www.gnu.org/software/gdb/documentation/>.

For help, type "help".

Type "apropos word" to search for commands related to "word".

(gdb) shell dir rangen_boost* /w

 Volume in drive C is SYSTEM

 Volume Serial Number is 8EA6-1DBE


 Directory of C:\CPP


rangen_boost.cpp        rangen_boost.exe        rangen_boost_gdb.exe

             3 File(s)         190,379 bytes

             0 Dir(s)   141,683,314,688 bytes free

(gdb) shell g++ -Wall -ansi -I ../boost_1_58_0 rangen_boost.cpp -o
rangen_boost_gdb_2 -g
```

```
(gdb) shell dir rangen_boost* /w
 Volume in drive C is SYSTEM
 Volume Serial Number is 8EA6-1DBE


 Directory of C:\CPP


rangen_boost.cpp          rangen_boost.exe
rangen_boost_gdb.exe
rangen_boost_gdb_2.exe
               4 File(s)           259,866 bytes
               0 Dir(s)   141,683,249,152 bytes free
```

In the preceding console output, we invoke the `dir` command to list all files that begin with the `rangen_boost` name within the active directory. Then, we invoke the compiling command to produce the `rangen_boost_gdb_2.exe` executable file in the active directory. Then, we call the `dir` command again to ensure that the `rangen_boost_gdb_2.exe` executable file has been successfully created.

[You can use the `apropos shell` command to get more information about shell command in GDB.]

Solving the error

In *Chapter 5, Delving into the Boost.Asio Library*, we discussed handling exception and error. If we follow all the source code in this book, we may never get any error code to confuse us. However, if we try to modify the source code, even just a little, an error code may be thrown for which the program will not give us any description. Since the error code thrown by the `Boost` library is based on Windows system error code and is beyond the scope of this book, we can find the description on **Microsoft Developer Network (MSDN)** website at `msdn.microsoft.com/en-us/library/windows/desktop/ms681381%28v=vs.85%29.aspx`. Here, we can find all translations of error codes from error 0 to 15999. Using GDB and error code translation from MSDN would become a powerful tool for solving an error that occurs in our program.

Let's go back to *Chapter 6, Creating a Client-server Application* and run the
serverasync program. When the program is run, it listens to the client in 127.0.0.1
on port 4444, which will be simulated by telnet in our example. However, what will
happen if the client is not responding? To know further, let's run the serverasync
program without running telnet. The following error will be displayed because the
client is not responding:

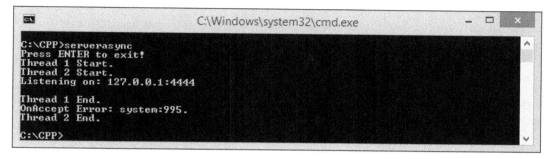

We got the system error code 995. Now, with this error code, we can visit MSDN
System Error Codes and find the error description, which is **The I/O operation has
been aborted because of either a thread exit or an application request. (ERROR_
OPERATION_ABORTED).**

What's next?

We are familiar with the basic GDB commands. There are many more commands in
GDB that we cannot discuss in this book. GDB has an official site that we can visit at
www.gnu.org/software/gdb/documentation/. Here, we can find all the complete
commands that we have not yet discussed.

 We can also get more detailed information on Boost C++
Libraries on the official website at www.boost.org,
especially for the Boost.Asio library documentation, which
is available at www.boost.org/doc/libs/1_58_0/doc/
html/boost_asio.html.

Summary

The debugging process is an essential thing that we can do to analyse our program by running it step-by-step. When our program produces unexpected results or it crashes in the middle of an execution, there is no other choice than to run the debugging process. GDB is our choice since it is compatible with the C++ language, as it comes with MinGW-w64 installer packages and is lightweight when loaded.

GDB can only run an executable file that compiles using the -g option. This option will add the debugging information and symbol, which are important in the debugging process. You will be unable to debug the executable files that are compiled without the -g option.

After we successfully load our program under GDB, we can choose either the run or start command to execute the debugging process. The run command will execute our program as usual but will stop if the debugger finds a breakpoint, while the start command will stop at the main block of program at the first execution.

When the debugger stops at certain line, we have to decide whether to continue the debugging process. We have the option to run the program until it exits or if the breakpoint is found using the continue command. Alternatively, we can run the debugger step-by-step using the next command.

To make the debugger stop at the execution of the debugging process, call the break [linenumber] command to set the breakpoint. If we want to ensure that we set the correct line number, call the list command to print the source code. Calling the delete N command will then delete the breakpoint where N can find the info break command.

Retrieving the value of a variable is also important when finding an error. If the program produces unexpected output, we can trace the value of a variable by printing it. We can do this by using the print [variablename] command. At the variable we suspect is causing an error, we can reassign the value of that variable with a new one using the set var [variablename] = [newvalue] command. We can then run the debugger again until we obtain the expected output. When we have fixed all the errors, and are sure that everything is perfect, we can recompile our program by calling the compiling command inside GDB prompt using the shell [Windows shell command] command.

Index

H

Hypertext Transfer Protocol (HTTP) 25, 132

I

Integrated Development Environment
    (IDE) 5, 157
Internet Assigned Numbers Authority
    (IANA)
  about 30
  URL 30
Internet Control Message Protocol
    (ICMP) 39
Internet Message Access Protocol
    (IMAP) 26
Internet Protocol
  about 31
  IPv4 32-34
  IPv6 35, 36
I/O object 71
I/O service
  dispatch() function, using 91-93
  examining, in Boost.Asio library 71
  handler, wrapping through strand
    object 102-104
  non-blocking poll() function, using 73, 74
  post() function, using 87-90
  run() function, blocking 71, 72
  run() function, using 71, 72
  serializing, with strand function 95-101
  threads, dealing with 77-79
  work object, removing 75, 76
ipconfig command
  about 37
  DNS, displaying 37, 38
  DNS, flushing 38
  full configuration information,
    displaying 37
  IP address, releasing 39
  IP address, renewing 39
iterators 50

L

list command 164
Logical Link Control (LLC) 22

M

Media Access Control (MAC) 22, 23
Message Passing Interface (MPI) 58
Microsoft Developer Network (MSDN)
  URL 170
MinGW compiler
  Boost C++ libraries, preparing 53
  setting up 1
MinGW-w64
  installing 2, 3
  URL 2
Minimalistic GNU for Windows
    (MinGW) 1

N

netstat command 45
networking systems
  about 21
  layer 21
  OSI reference model 22
  protocol 21
  TCP/IP reference model 27
Network layer, OSI reference model 24
next command 162
non-blocking poll() function
  using 73, 74
nonconcurrent programming
  versus concurrent programming 68-70
non-copyable error 83
Notepad++
  URL 5

O

OSI reference model
  about 22
  Application layer 25, 26
  Data Link layer 22, 23
  Network layer 24
  Physical layer 22
  Presentation layer 25
  Session layer 24
  Transport layer 24

P

Path environment
about 3
setting up 3, 4
pathping command 43-45
physical address 22
Physical layer, OSI reference model 22
ping command 40, 41
ports
about 30, 31
port number 30
post() function
using 87-90
Post Office Protocol (POP3) 26
Presentation layer, OSI reference model 25
Pseudorandom Number Generator
(PRNG) 61

R

Round Trip Time (RTT) 43
run() function
blocking 71, 72
using 71, 72

S

Session layer, OSI reference model
communication methods 24, 25
share_ptr pointer
URL 76
Simple Network Management Protocol
(SNMP) 26
socket
OnRecv() function, using 147
OnSend() function, using 146
reading 140-146
Recv() function, using 147
Send() function, using 146
writing 140-146
Standard Template Library (STL)
about 49
algorithms 50
containers 50

example 50-52
iterators 50
start command 161
step command 162
strand function
using 96-101
synchronous process 68

T

TCP/IP reference model
about 27
layers 27
TCP/IP tools, for troubleshooting
about 37
ipconfig command 37
netstat command 45, 46
pathping command 43-45
ping command 39-41
telnet command 47, 48
tracert command 42, 43
Text Editor
installing 5
selecting 5
threads
dealing with 76-79
timer
creating, with timer class 116
expiring 116-118
using, with boost::bind function 119-122
using, with boost::strand function 123-126
Transmission Control Protocol (TCP)
about 28, 29
acknowledge (ACK) flags 28
Cyclical Redundancy Check (CRC) 29
negative acknowledge (NACK) packet 29
sliding window 29
synchronize (SYN) flag 28
Transport layer, OSI reference model
Transmission Control Protocol (TCP) 24
User Datagram Protocol (UDP) 24
Trivial FTP (TFTP) 25

U

User Datagram Protocol (UDP) 29, 30

V

vector 51
Visual Studio 157
Voice over IP (VoIP) 30

W

work object
  removing 75, 76

Thank you for buying
Boost.Asio C++ Network Programming
Second Edition

About Packt Publishing

Packt, pronounced 'packed', published its first book, *Mastering phpMyAdmin for Effective MySQL Management*, in April 2004, and subsequently continued to specialize in publishing highly focused books on specific technologies and solutions.

Our books and publications share the experiences of your fellow IT professionals in adapting and customizing today's systems, applications, and frameworks. Our solution-based books give you the knowledge and power to customize the software and technologies you're using to get the job done. Packt books are more specific and less general than the IT books you have seen in the past. Our unique business model allows us to bring you more focused information, giving you more of what you need to know, and less of what you don't.

Packt is a modern yet unique publishing company that focuses on producing quality, cutting-edge books for communities of developers, administrators, and newbies alike. For more information, please visit our website at www.packtpub.com.

About Packt Open Source

In 2010, Packt launched two new brands, Packt Open Source and Packt Enterprise, in order to continue its focus on specialization. This book is part of the Packt Open Source brand, home to books published on software built around open source licenses, and offering information to anybody from advanced developers to budding web designers. The Open Source brand also runs Packt's Open Source Royalty Scheme, by which Packt gives a royalty to each open source project about whose software a book is sold.

Writing for Packt

We welcome all inquiries from people who are interested in authoring. Book proposals should be sent to author@packtpub.com. If your book idea is still at an early stage and you would like to discuss it first before writing a formal book proposal, then please contact us; one of our commissioning editors will get in touch with you.

We're not just looking for published authors; if you have strong technical skills but no writing experience, our experienced editors can help you develop a writing career, or simply get some additional reward for your expertise.

open source *
community experience distilled

Boost.Asio C++ Network
Programming

Boost.Asio C++ Network Programming

ISBN: 978-1-78216-326-8   Paperback: 156 pages

Enhance your skills with practical examples for C++
network programming

1.   Augment your C++ network programming
     using Boost.Asio.

2.   Discover how Boost.Asio handles synchronous
     and asynchronous programming models.

3.   Practical examples of client/server applications.

4.   Learn how to deal with threading when writing
     network applications.

Getting Started with C++ Audio
Programming for Game Development

Getting Started with C++ Audio Programming for Game Development

ISBN: 978-1-84969-909-9   Paperback: 116 pages

A hands-on guide to audio programming in game
development with the FMOD audio library and
toolkit

1.   Add audio to your game using FMOD and
     wrap it in your own code.

2.   Understand the core concepts of audio
     programming and work with audio at different
     levels of abstraction.

3.   Work with a technology that is widely
     considered to be the industry standard in audio
     middleware.

Please check **www.PacktPub.com** for information on our titles

Advanced Quantitative Finance with C++

ISBN: 978-1-78216-722-8   Paperback: 124 pages

Create and implement mathematical models in C++ using Quantitative Finance

1. Describes the key mathematical models used for price equity, currency, interest rates, and credit derivatives.

2. The complex models are explained step-by-step along with a flow chart of every implementation.

3. Illustrates each asset class with fully solved C++ examples, both basic and advanced, that support and complement the text.

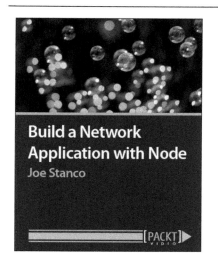

Build a Network Application with Node [Video]

ISBN: 978-1-78216-827-0   Duration: 02:20 hours

Build, tune, and test a tangible Node.js application from start to finish

1. Offers the reader a primer in node conventions, along with best practices for publishing modules, optimizing performance, and organizing code.

2. Step-by-step examples that demonstrate how to progressively enhance your app.

Please check **www.PacktPub.com** for information on our titles

CPSIA information can be obtained
at www.ICGtesting.com
Printed in the USA
LVHW101915010221
678032LV00007B/639